NEW VISIONS
FOR
BLACK MEN

Na'im Akbar, Ph.D.

MIND

PRODUCTIONS

First printing January 2017

Cover Design: Ashleigh Beverly, *The Dezignher, LLC.*

Published by Mind Productions & Associates, Inc.
Tallahassee, FL 32304

ISBN: 978-1-5136-1373-4
Printed in the United States of America

Dedication

For the men and future men of my lineage:
"Pa Bud" (Thomas Weems), Grandfather
"My Daddy" (Luther B. Weems), My Father

My sons:
Mutaqee Na'im Akbar
Tareeq Nashid Akbar

Grandsons:
Hasaan, Mylles . . . . (those unborn)

. . . and some men who walked with me while gaining my vision:

Syed Khatib*
DuBois Phillip McGee*
Wade Nobles
Asa Hilliard*
Louis Farrakhan
Benson George Cooke
Dawud Akbar*
Maulana Karenga
Kobi Kambon
Jackie Mayfield
Abdul Shakir
Na'im Majeed
Molefi Asante
Tony Browder
Lester Bentley
John Henrik Clarke*
W. D. Mohammed*
Johnny R. Youngblood
Joseph McMillan*
Paul Hasan

Willie Wilson
R. B. Holmes, Jr.
Chester Grundy
Armiya Nu'Man*
Ivan Van Sertima*
George Fraser
Nashid Fakriddeen
Jacob Carruthers*
Morris F. X. Jeff*
Jeremiah Wright
Tavis Smiley
Jerome Schiele
Eric P. Abercrumbie
William R. Jones*
Josef ben Jochannon*
Alvin Turner
Leonard Jeffries
Dick Gregory
Adib A. Shakir

*Ancestors

Contents

Introduction

--The right time, the right place, the right author.--

It is my distinct honor and pleasure to offer introductory words to the updated version of a book that changed my life written by a man that inspired a people. I read Visions for Black Men in 1992 as a sophomore at Morehouse College while taking a Black psychology class. The fact that Dr. Akbar was a professor at Morehouse during the 1970's and that we both went to the University of Michigan for graduate school established a virtual connection with him in my mind about which he did not know until several years later. Over the past decade, I have included Dr. Akbar's model of "males to boys to men" in several of the presentations and workshops with young Black males and the teachers, parents, and other adults that interact with and care for them. The principles are timeless, but I am ecstatic that he is releasing New Visions to introduce the model and his insights to a new generation of Black males.

Divine timing never ceases to amaze. At the writing of New Visions for Black Men, Black men serve as the President of the United States, Secretary of Homeland Security, Secretary of Education, Secretary of Transportation, and up until very recently, the Attorney General. There are over 35,000 African American millionaires (male and female combined), three African American billionaires (Robert Smith, Michael Jordan, and Oprah Winfrey). More African American males have health care, high school diplomas and college degrees than at any other time in U.S. history and despite still woefully disparate incarceration rates for Black males there has begun a slow but steady decline.

Although these facts sound good on the surface, let's add some context. President Obama passed significant healthcare legislation during the very small 4.5-month window (late September, 2009 through early February, 2010) at the beginning of his first term in office working with a majority of democrats in the U.S. House of Representatives and sixty democrats in the Senate. Outside of that window, however, Republicans contested almost every piece of legislation that President Obama proposed, some of which would have significantly helped the African American community. Although there were four Black men holding secretary positions in 2015, President Obama appointed roughly the same number of African Americans to cabinet positions as George W. Bush and a lower number than Bill Clinton (although President Obama appointed a higher percentage of Black federal judges than Bush or Clinton). Although we have 35,000 Black millionaires, there actually should be 300,000 given the size of the African American population and we should have seventy rather than three Black billionaires. The statistics in health care, education, and incarceration are better than in previous years, but significant gaps with White Americans remain. To say this is the best of times and worst of times for African Americans does not seem appropriate. Rather, this seems to be the slightly better of times and the "it could be worse of times."

The brilliance of New Visions is that it provides a framework and language that exposes Black people (and those who care about them) to the specific knowledge, skills, attitudes, and behaviors necessary to improve their lives. Applying the vernacular of the book to the aforementioned statistics and observations, the male would say "it's cool that we have a Black president", the boy would ask, "what has the Black president done for me?", but the man would ask, "what can the Black president do for us and how can we help him?" This book challenges the reader, regardless of race and gender, to engage in an introspective set of questions that will fundamentally include, "Am I a man (or woman)?"

To explore human development through the lens of the Black male is not only timely, it is extremely appropriate in the context of America. Whether it is health, income, education, incarceration, societal perceptions, or life expectancy, Black males have more negative life outcomes than any other racial/gender group with the exception of Native Americans living on reservations. Within the two years preceding the release of New Visions, several Black males, many unarmed, have died at the hands of police officers. Many of these incidents were videotaped and viewed by millions of Americans and people around the world. The list of victims and the states in which the incidents occurred includes but is not limited to: Eric Garner (NY), John Crawford (OH), Michael Brown (MO), Tamir Rice (OH), Walter Scott (SC), Freddie Gray (MD), Ezell Ford (CA), Alton Sterling (LA), and Philando Castile (MN). Videotapes notwithstanding, less than 3% of police that killed Blacks males (many of whom were unarmed) have been convicted.

Males and boys will not have the self-knowledge, selflessness, confidence, independence, and commitment to justice and their people to speak truth to power regarding the unjust killing of young Black males, but men do. While some males and boys may forward a Black Lives Matter quote or march in a protest, which they see more as a fun activity that everyone else is doing than a demonstration of deep conviction, the man will compliment marching with political, economic, and spiritual strategies designed to improve conditions for the masses over the long term. Men vote. Men read. Men create. Men organize. Men pray. Men are disciplined. Men engage in the hard and sacrificial work that leads to progress, even when they know they will not see the full fruit of their labor.

In the face of negative societal challenges and negative outcomes, many Black men have transitioned from the maleness of the caterpillar to the boyhood of the cocoon to the manhood of the butterfly. The analogy of the caterpillar-cocoon-butterfly metamorphosis used in New Visions is a vivid and compelling illustration of development that allows the Black male to envision himself in three distinct but naturally progressive stages. It allows him to realize that just as there is butterfly potential in the caterpillar, there is manhood potential in the male. The ability for Black men to excel personally, socially, professionally, and spiritually in spite of an adverse and obstacle-laden environment is the epitome of the American dream. His success, which should be statistically improbable, needs to be appreciated and studied by anyone who cares about optimal human development.

Although modern Black males face challenges of many stripes, Dr. Akbar methodically describes the lives, challenges, and victories of Moses and Jesus to illustrate the divine hand that guides the steps of fully developed men. He then provides more recent examples of Black men via the narratives and achievements of Marcus Garvey, W.E.B. Dubois, Elijah Muhammad, Martin Luther King, Jr., and Paul Robeson amongst others. The clear message is that these men, through a variety of experiences, developed into men during periods of blatant oppression, racism, and having enemies who were visible and unapologetic in their Pharoah/Herod-like opposition. These men, in the tradition of other great African men, felt justifiably entitled to be human. They are the Imhotep, Ramses II, Akhenaton and Mansa Musa's of the modern era. As the first people to exist, and think, and create civilization, the African man has more experience with being a man than anyone else. He is the first manifestation of God in the flesh, and as such, he should never feel subservient or second to anyone else. It is my deepest hope and expectation that this book will inspire and challenge modern Black men to reach true butterfly manhood as it has for me.

Peace and Blessings
Rev. Dr. Bryant T. Marks, Sr.
Atlanta, GA
July 10, 2016

Foreword

I first met Dr. Na'im Akbar the summer of 1994. I was president of the University of Toledo Black Student Union and working for a program called Toledo EXCEL. The program was taking nearly two dozen high school students on an ambitious cultural and academic expedition to Ghana West Africa and "Doc" (as I would refer to him years later) was the lead US academician providing instruction during our courses at the University of Ghana at Legon. I watched as Dr. Akbar navigated with ease both the intellectual engagement of students during the day and the psychological support of young spirits during evening mentoring. It was during this experience I realized that I wanted more exposure to and tutelage from this giant spirit.

Upon returning to the states I immediately picked up Visions For Black Men, published only three years before I cracked its simplistically bold cover. The book spoke to me immediately. I tore through its pages, convicted, inspired, informed, and directed. I had a dad that was present in my life and a village of men who had invested in me. But no previous instruction presented such deep insight into the psyche of black men, the historical realities that impacted our present situation, or the unapologetic accountability required to become a man. My problem at that time is that I was 20, arrogant, rebellious against being mentored, budding talent potential, but had not created an ecosystem of elders to guide me or developed friendships that welcomed the kind of transparent engagement that helps men cultivate each other in a better way. I was a boy trying to guide myself through a manhood curriculum. As a result, this early phase of my development was a short lived process.

It would be nearly a decade before I picked up Visions again for personal use. It was a terrible personal moment. I was in the midst of a divorce; was an inconsistent dad; and was in a crisis of character. This time I cracked open Akbar's work looking to discover what my own vision of Manhood was. I was immediately forced to look into a mirror; and the reflection staring back at me was that of a grown ass boy pretending to be a man. Chapter by chapter I acknowledged personal flaws and developed strategies to address them. Chapter by chapter I saw the errors I'd made in establishing and operating in relationships and began to see new ways to love. Finally, I constructed a vision for manhood that was divinely connected to my purpose on earth and started walking towards it. I haven't stopped. Visions For Black Men became the lifeline that helped me go beyond the rhetoric of manhood and dared me to develop a manhood strategy. Nearly another decade has passed; I'm in a wonderful marriage, love my daily interaction with my children and even in my imperfection see a MAN in the mirror I am proud of, using his gifts to enrich his family and the world.

You may be asking why I'm talking so much about myself and not the book. I have come to realize that books are empty words if the instruction on the pages doesn't lead the reader to transformation. I am more equipped to tell you about my own transformation than I am anyone else's. But it was MY very transformation (aided by Visions) that led me to use the book as I assisted brothers in going through their own journey. For years it was my go to text when I spoke to boys and men about self development, manhood, and the strength found in the relationships of real men. One day that recommendation was televised for millions of people on the OWN Network's "Iyanla Fix My Life", program. I was asked by Iyanla Vanzant to speak to some brothers who had multiple children with multiple mothers and were struggling with who they were and wanted to become. At one point in the show I mentioned Dr. Akbar and Visions. I provided a summation of his teachings on the developmental stages of the "Male, Boy, and Man." I further confessed how I and so many had been boys dressed like men, ruining our lives and those relying on us to be real men.

Several of the fathers on the show immediately related to the reference, and one even acknowledged his failure to operate as a man specifically in his relationships with women. You would have thought I wrote the book, as hundreds of brothers reached out to me asking for the title of the book I'd mentioned on Iyanla. Scores of women contacted me via social media to say they too wanted to read Visions or buy it for a loved one. But the correspondence I was most excited by came from Dr. Akbar's son; communicating the increase in requests for the book and if I was open to speaking with Doc.
Writing this forward is the completion of a circle. As men we are often presented with information that inspires us, but doesn't motivate us to move. We are often led to move, but lack the support and

mentorship required to truly evolve. Still many men have the inspiration and motivation coupled with instruction, but have never built a circle of accountability that ensures that they are surrounded by men to encourage their best potential and not boys that validate their weakness and immaturity. I can tell you that Visions was one of the many tools I needed to begin a journey of Manhood that has and I pray will never end.

Dr. Akbar's New Visions is poised to enlighten both boys trying to develop their vision of what manhood will be for them, as well as men looking for an evolved since of self. As you read this reimagined Visions for Black Men, imagine, seek, embrace and claim your best self. That man inside you longing to live in the light of day. He walks in imperfect character, defying hate in order to personify love and recognizing that the true testament of every man lies in something infinitely more powerful than a title or bank account; but in our LEGACY--the one that we build every day with each decision. What's the Vision you have for your Legacy Black Man? Now is the Time to build!

Jeffrey Johnson, CEO
JIJ Communications
Cleveland, OH
July 2016

Introduction
(1991 EDITION)

Much has been written and spoken in recent years regarding the "crisis" of the African-American man. He has been characterized as an "endangered species," a victim of "genocide," the "most vulnerable American," and a variety of other catastrophic descriptions. The rhetoric of this condition of this condition is second only to the awesome statistics and painful facts which illustrate the most unfortunate circumstance of black men in America. No rational person who is aware of these facts could with any claim to sanity minimize this situation. It is vital that we assess the situation of the African American man within an historical and spiritually sound context.

In fact, the crisis of the African male in America began with the landing of the first slave ship in the vicinity of four hundred years ago. This crisis has had varying levels of intensity throughout our recent history in North America interacting with the conquerors from Europe. If we mean by "crisis": the critical turning point in a situation with specific reference to life-threatening circumstances, then we have been in a perpetual state of crisis. The millions of African people who died in the middle passage and the subsequent millions who died from abuse and neglect on the plantation certainly constitute a crisis. When we recount the mutilations, murders, dismemberment, violent beatings and inhuman brutal abuse, we see a crisis. When we recall the terror of intimidation and psychological dismemberment, we see a crisis. When we are reminded of the destruction to family units, culture, intellect, spiritual concepts, the human degradation and the centuries of terrorist attacks against Africans in America, there is no other way to understand these conditions except as persistent life-threatening and murderous conditions.

In many ways, the tendency to focus on the contemporary status of African-American men as a particular crisis fails to appreciate the full context of the history of African people in America. Such failure deprives us of some important facts in our past which influence our present situation. It also permits a partially blind analysis to blame the victim and abdicate the responsibility of the perpetrator of these conditions. Even more importantly, by ignoring the full historical context of these present conditions, we fail to take note of the very significant fact that the survival of African people under these extraordinary conditions is a phenomenon of miraculous proportions. The fact that we still have casualties as a result of this unrelenting attack on African humanness and life is far from an incidental event. With the on-going economic, educational, psychological, political, even military assault on Black life, there is no wonder that we have prisoners of the war—poor, uninformed, self-destructive and confused people. Whatever modern techniques of warfare that might characterize this attack on Black men, the conditions are essentially unchanged for the fallen dead and dying, whether in hubs of slave ships, on Southern plantations, in police-infected urban ghettoes, on AIDS deathbeds or on death row in the prisons of America. Death is death and death has been a constant companion to the Black man (and woman) throughout the African encounter with Europeans.

Black resilience and apparent stubborn determination to survive and thrive are nothing short of a miracle. It would be most informative to assess the potential for anything approaching the African victory over oppression with other human beings on the planet. We were never intended to survive in America and our survival has been in direct defiance of the most consistent, brutal and devastating attack on human life in the modern history of humanity. The fact that African people continue to produce exceedingly effective human beings whose intellect, talents, --and most importantly, their human sensitivity and moral life—have remained intact is nothing less than clear evidence of Divine intervention in modern history.

When problems are analyzed and approached with the essential focus on the negative then the solutions will invariably be "reactions" rather than "actions." Reactions lock you in the construct of the problem. If we look at what's wrong to the exclusion of attending to a model of success, health and solutions then the consequence will be a social theory written out of despair and modeled on disturbance rather than Truth. This approach to experiences will be a constant state of correction rather than reconstruction or restoration of an order that affirms our progress as human beings. This means that we build a society with nothing more than a few handouts to address transitory crisis intervention, remedial programs, methadone treatments, larger prisons, more effective crime control, drugs for human restraint and politics of compromise. This is not the stuff that human progress is made of. Human progress requires a vision. This vision must be of an idealized form of how things ought to be, with the focus on the best concept of the potentials of the group involved. It must be based on a vivid and exalted concept of what those people have been at their best. It must be drawn from a metaphysical conception of the order to the universe. It must incorporate the triumphs over encounters with disordered life forms and it must have s sustained conception of the resurrecting, regenerative, and transformative nature of human existence.

This vision for black men must have several elements. On the one hand, it must be panoramic in its integration of ancient and pre-European intervention in the African experience; the experience of the American holocaust (i.e. enslavement of African people; the consequences of white supremacy and racism and the contemporary European-American socialization. The impact of each of these components must be considered in any thorough analysis of the condition of Black Men. It must break away from the traditional social science conceptions of linear time (i.e., events moving systematically from past to present towards the future) with present causative factors being most influential. It must consider that life events and causative factors cannot be gleaned from observations of the immediate circumstances, but must take account the interplay of multiple and metaphysical causation (future reality can determine present and past events). Such logic is rather alien to Western scientific and metaphysical reality, while it is captured in Divine scriptures and in the folk traditions of most of the peoples on the earth. It is particularly relevant to understanding the cosmos from the vantage point of African people or "Africentricity."

The vision must also be holistic. It must take into account physical/material realities, mental/social realities and spiritual/moral realities. Such holistic thinking is difficult for people deeply entrenched in the Western approach to knowledge, primarily a system of analysis that prides itself in its ability to break things down, compartmentalize them, and gain mastery through focus on the fragments. Western specialization is both its greatest strength and its greatest flaw. The fact that they have social scientists with no spiritual consciousness has produced a breed of morally retarded manipulators of human life. The fact that their medical personnel are experts on the body has made them inadequate healers because of their failure to take into account the interaction of the mind and the soul in the processes of dis-ease as well as healing.

This African vision for black men must include the full dimensions of human experience and understand that there is no event which does not have simultaneous and systematic impact on other systems of existence. The body does not even experience tension that is not simultaneously registered in the mental and spiritual spheres. Spiritual issues cannot be cannot be easily observed outside of some material expression, whether acknowledged or not. A mind operating in a body improperly nourished is deficient, as a body operating with a mind inadequately conscious is handicapped. There is no science without a moral reference and the visible always has parallels which are invisible. What is tangible is only a reflection of a higher intangible reality. What is perceived as immediate is only a link in a chain of perceived causation. A vision must be comprehensive if it will serve the role of initiating revolutionary occurrence.

Because we conceive this vision for black men within an Africentric context, we have incorporated the elements discussed above. Our data moves seamlessly from the insights of Eurocentric social science to the imagery of religious scriptures. It utilizes poetry, allegory and rhetoric with the same facility as it utilizes the empirical evidence of the senses. It draws upon the power of symbols, myths and imagery as liberally as it draws upon quantification and classification. The objective is to chart a course formed out of the natural expression and experience of African people. The idea is to view an aspect of our experience—the reality of being black men—from the full range of what is considered real by the ancient criteria of science as established by African minds long ago.

This is the only way that we can build a proactive vision for ourselves which draws upon our strengths rather than our weaknesses. This is the only way that we can move beyond seeing ourselves as endangered victims and seeing ourselves as agents of self-determining creators of change. This is the only way that we can begin to conceptualize our reality from the vantage point of our own center rather than being the exceptional case on the non-normative scale of someone else's continuum of reality. Our vision must take us beyond where we are to achieve a new and higher state; we must conceive a new and higher state in a new and higher way.

In anticipation of my critics, it is rather important that I make several disclaimers. This collection of ideas focuses on the plight of black men and deals with those issues in an isolated way (which actually contradicts one of my essential principles about being holistic and contextual when analyzing issues.) We assume from the outset that men and women are inextricably tied together and fully equal in all aspects of their fundamental humanity. The conditions affecting the lives of African men and women (in fact, all men and women are inseparable. Though the images and illustrations in this discussion focus on African-American men, there is no assumption that these issues are gender specific and do not have a comparable impact on women. The prophetic vision though phrased in masculine terms is not a "men-only" vision, but a vision for African people as a whole and ultimately a vision for the highest expression for the entirety of those who choose to be authentically human. So this is not an exclusive, elitist, racist or sexist vision. It focuses on a particular in order to speak to some universals.

We do, however, contend that there are some unique problems that black men and women face differentially. We recognize that certain problems which occur in greater prevalence among one of the other of the sexes is, again the expression the symptoms of a more global problem. Because of the limitations of language and the compartmentalization of logic and Western thought in general there are inevitable confusions and dichotomies that may be implied, but not intended. We implore the reader to be sensitive to these difficulties and to attribute to the writer biases and inhibitions that are the legacy from deficiencies in the system and language that we are forced to use.

Finally, I must extend personal thanks to Abdul Shakir, who prodded and assisted me in this project and whose help was invaluable. My office staff, (Gloria Mu'min, Troy Council and Andrew Gray) was the muscle behind getting this done. There are hundreds of people who made possible the presentations out of which these essays emerged and whose inspiration and insistence kept me working on the project. My thanks to all of them, my family and the ancestral spirit who serve as agents of the Almighty, whose benevolence has permitted all.

Peace be with you,
Na'im Akbar
Tallahassee, Florida
January 25, 1991

1

From Maleness to Manhood

A more complete title for this section should be: "From Maleness to Manhood: The Transformation of the African-American Consciousness, or For Colored Boys Who Have Considered Homicide When Manhood was Enough." Unfortunately, we take as a given that despite superficial changes, America has been, still is and very probably will be for some time to come, a striving, sturdy, racist society. Sadly, we have seen over the course of the last two hundred years that from the Halls of Congress to the unemployment lines there is clear evidence that racism is the predictable American way. Race is a better predictor of the course of your life, than anything else. Even though we accept the realities of racism and racial oppression, we submit that all of these problems and challenges that consume so much of our energy and attention may, in fact, be only symptomatic of something more basic that affects us that has not been resolved. We also want to suggest the possibility that there is a weapon available to us, that is within us, that has not been fully developed, which if developed could perhaps eliminate many of the consequences of the challenges and problems that we confront as an oppressed community.

The Process of Transformation

The Ancient Scholars of classical African civilization identified the nature of the human being as one in a continuous state of evolution or on-going development. This evolution or continuous transformation is not unlike what is seen as happening in all aspects of nature all of the time. A high pressure air mass, under the correct circumstances transforms into a storm, a tornado or even perhaps a hurricane. Winds moving at certain velocities collide with air of certain temperatures will be transformed into even another type of storm or maybe, will be blown away into nothingness. We know that a worm-like creature that crawls on plants in the form of a leaf-eating caterpillar, in the appointed time and under the proper conditions will spin a cocoon, confine itself and will eventually be transformed from a slimy, hairy, crawling life form and emerge as a beautiful and colorful creature capable of flying with celestial beauty. Transformation can be seen in all parts of the natural world around us and it is also a characteristic of the human being as well. The distinction between the caterpillar and the human is that if the caterpillar does not undergo its transformation into a butterfly, it will die in the form of a worm. It is programmed to become its completed self or meet an untimely death. The difference with the human being is that he can live in his "worm-like" form and die in that form with no evidence of any greater possibility. Humans never have to become fully human and can live a life for many years and neither he nor other incompletely formed worm-like humans will ever know that they did not become completed human beings. We can live and die and raise other worm-like humans for generations and never discover our true humanity. In fact, humans actually can recognize the potential in the human make-up and with their free will can choose not to become a "butterfly human." Entire civilizations can boast about their inhumanity while observing the true possibilities of being human by observing other fully developed humans. As the famous English writer, William Shakespeare, declared in one of his famous plays (Hamlet): ". . . . To be or not to be, that is the question."

The point of this discussion is that we all have the potential to become fully human! Knowledge and choice are the keys, since unlike the insect that has its butterfly potential automatically programmed into its nature, we must be taught and then select to become fully human. The human being is transformed by his thinking and not by his diet and his physical environment as is the case with the caterpillar that becomes a butterfly or simply dies. The lesson of human transformation must be learned and our power for self-determination must be applied in order for us to become the fully developed human being we were born to become. Another image that we gain from studying the butterfly demonstrates another benefit of transformation. While in the worm state, it is subjected to a wide range of dangers from the environment: the foot of a human being can smash it; or eating the wrong kinds of poisonous leaves can kill it in the early stages of its growth process; strong winds can blow it off of the tree that it feeds; spider webs might entrap it and immobilize it as prey and a variety of other environmental hazards. However when the worm has made its transformation, it can fly above the same body with a careless foot that might have smashed it; it can use the winds that formerly tossed it from its perch as a vehicle to enhance its travel; it can soar above the web that might have entrapped him as a worm and feed from heights that its earth-bound prey could never reach.

This image not only demonstrates the potential of transformation, it demonstrates the benefits of being transformed into ones completed form as a butterfly or a completed human being. The butterfly has much greater mastery over the potential dangers to its survival than the more humble caterpillar that is much more vulnerable and at the mercy of the dangers of a lower nature. The butterfly is still subject to dangers from its environment, but it is much better equipped to avoid many of the dangers of its lower form. The analogy is that when we are transformed into "Men" or our higher human form, we are in a stronger state of self-determination than we were as "boys" or in our lower human form as "males." With this picture in mind, we are going to describe the transformation of the human being as an illustration of the benefits of transformation of African consciousness (human thought) moving from the lowly level of maleness, to boyishness to manhood.

What Is a Male?

The beginning stage of development is that of being simply a Male. What are the characteristics of this Male? A Male is a biological entity whose essence and awareness is described by no more or no less than his physical anatomy, drives, emotions and make-up. One need not look beyond the observable anatomical characteristics, primarily his genitals, to determine his maleness. This fact of being male is usually established at conception and is observable at birth (or somewhat earlier with some of the more sophisticated modern medical equipment such as a sonogram.) There is no controversy that this entity is of male gender. This male characterization is a predetermined fact of the biological life which is in no way subject to choice. (Let's be very clear that "gender", which is a physical event and "sexuality", which is a psychological or social event, is not the same thing and this discussion is about physical characteristics of gender.) At this level of being, the male child's make-up is just like that of the caterpillar, that is, it is determined by nature. Of course, we are aware that genetic engineering is increasingly at the level that it is capable of even making gender a choice, but once conceived, there are certain physical characteristics locked into the biological make-up. We are also aware that there are certain rare occurrences of nature that result in transgender characteristics, that result in both male and female genitals being evident in the physical make-up, but usually the biology is clear in distinguishing the genitals that determine the gender of the child that is identified as "male."

Maleness is not only a predetermined biological characteristic of this gender of the species; there is also a basic level of awareness, consciousness or mentality that corresponds with the same principles that correspond with that developmental level of the biology. (These characteristics are not in contrast to being of the female gender; our discussion is about the male, but the mentality of the female gender is pretty much the same.) This level of awareness or mentality is one predominated by instincts, urges, desires or feelings. The "male" or most primitive mindset is, just like the body: driven by the relief of tension and the satisfaction of basic urges or desires. At this stage of development, when the bladder is filled, the Male child does not say, "Momma, may I relieve myself in the bathroom?" He simply empties his bladder by wetting on Momma or whoever, or whatever may be in the way of the release of the tension from a filled bladder. In other words he pees on the spot until the pressure is relieved. When the male creature experiences the urge to eat, he does not have the mindset that can calm him from panic by saying to his mind or awareness: "If I am simply patient, someone will take care of this urge and bring me something to eat soon." His consciousness is one of immediate panic to the discomfort that is experienced as, "I want to eat right now, to stop this discomfort or I will die!" Neither does the male have the consideration or knowledge to look at the clock and realize that it is 2:00 a.m. and his exhausted caretakers who just fed him a short while ago are trying to get some rest. Such details are not a part of the driven self-concerned instinct of the male mentality. It doesn't have a concept in its mind of "later" or someone else's needs. The survival instinct of the male mentality is guided by the "appetite monster" that works on the principle of "I want it, when I want it!" he experiences any kind of need. "NOW" is the only dimension of time it knows.

This "Male Mentality" is also driven by high octane passion which results from the release of tension and the panic that goes with the pressure of "want." Passion is an intense desire for pleasure or to have its needs satisfied. There is no concept in the male's head that suggests: "I will restrain myself and endure this discomfort for a moment because I really will not die." Neither does passion permit the male awareness to process the idea that, "I can change my position and reduce my discomfort;" or " if I share this toy that I have as Momma has told me to do, it will increase my pleasure by satisfying Momma." There is a greed that underlies the passion of the male mentality to receive all of the pleasure it can get, for itself alone without delay. Whatever brings pleasure to the Male Mentality, he wants as much of it as he can manage to consume, as often as he can get to it. The Male mind wants all of it, all the time.

Another characteristic of the "Male Mentality" is his dependency. Since this level of biological development limits what he can do for himself, the mentality that goes with it is one of expecting someone else to do everything for him all of the time. When someone comes along and sticks a nipple into his mouth that is craving the passionate pleasure of having hunger pains removed, he experiences some degree of temporary satisfaction. He may even swoon away into slumber with the pleasure that he experiences with having his panic removed. Similarly, the male is not capable of cleaning himself up. He experiences the fleeting pleasure of letting "poop" out of his bowels and laying there in it until someone comes along to relieve the newly engineered mess that he created. The male mentality is driven by hunger, greed, passion and an ever growing demand that someone should satisfy his demands and restore him to comfort. He is in this state of mind, a whining, crying, demanding, and dependent little "leech." This description is rather judgmental and represents a view from a later stage. It's not unlike the unpleasant repulsion that one is likely to have to the creepy, crawling, hairy worm in the form of the caterpillar. We are aware that these characteristics are very appropriate for the survival of the creatures at the earliest stages of their lives at the origin of its development. This behavior is expected, tolerated and actually, encouraged by caretakers at the infancy of the male stage. Any young male that doesn't demonstrate these demanding characteristics is likely to get a swift visit to the emergency room, if it doesn't manifest these qualities at the appropriate time at the origin of life. Parents are sure to panic if their newborn male is not passionate, demanding, whining, insatiable in its needs and desirous of being cuddled dependently. In its time and at its stage, this "male mentality" is not only appropriate but instructive. It is the young organism's introduction to interacting with the outside world, expressing its needs with conviction and having the humility to express its dependence on others. In its place, the Male Mentality is of great benefit in laying the foundation for the formation of the real "Man." In the wrong time, these same behaviors can become distasteful, destructive and deformed, blocking transformation into true Manhood. Not unlike the caterpillar that must eat constantly in that stage of development, it must eventually begin to form its cocoon to enter into transformation to become the butterfly or be destroyed if it gets stuck in this developmental stage.

Stuck in the "Male Stage"

What are some of the characteristics of an entire community whose minds are stuck in the "Male Stage" of development? One characteristic of such people is their belief that someone else has the responsibility to take care of them and satisfy their basic needs. Their essential approach to life is: "Feed me; put a roof over my head; take care of my basic survival needs. The expectation of these "beings" that are stuck in the dependency orientation from the male stage is: "Give me what I need." The nature of this mind is in a constant state of begging. They feel entitled to be taken care of by someone else. They have a greedy, hungry mind that constantly wants more and sees the only way to get it is asking for a hand-out. They respond with panic when their caretakers withdraw their resources. They will whine and cry in despair and anger because they believe that they are incapable of generating the kind of resources that could begin to provide for themselves. They are indignant when the caretakers take away their food stamps, close down the schools for their children and force them into a state of self-determination to look after themselves. "Give me back my baby formula or breast milk . . . . Gimme . . . . . . Gimme !" This mind operates with instant panic from a position of instinct and impulse. Since they are striking out in fear and panic they do not consider the consequences of their actions. When this male mentality sees something that arouses its appetite, it immediately goes into a begging posture, trying to have it given to them. The "male mentality" at whatever age it occurs, deals with all of its appetites in the same way, whether it's for food, sexual gratification and anything that brings it pleasure. The attractive person that arouses the male's sexual appetite could be someone else's mate, or even a defenseless juvenile. "Desire" is in control and passion drives the action. With a mind operating from the level of the "male stage' there is no ability to make any meaningful discriminating decisions. The male drive can't ask the question of whether the desired person smells bad or not. There is no capacity to raise objections or qualifications and definitely no ability to consider the consequences of their actions. The male appetite is consumed by its own desires of the moment without considering that he or the object of his desire might get shot and killed by someone for acting on his desire. "No, I am driven by passion so I reach out and feel you on the behind. I am just a "male." The male defines himself by his anatomical protrusion (or penis) and then experiences greater self worth by the volume, the depth, the length and the activity of that anatomical protrusion. As just a "male", one is essentially no more than a "dangling piece of flesh" located about five inches below the navel.

These rather crude descriptions are hopefully disturbing to the many chronologically mature persons who consider themselves to be men, yet find images of themselves in these descriptions of the "male mentality." Our intention is quite clear in these graphic pictures of the "male at work". If these qualities sound like you and your actions you are probably (quite literally) stuck in your "worm" stage of development. When we think only as males, then we operate only as flesh creatures. Though our subject in this discussion is the development of the man, it's important that women understand that if they operate only as "females" then they will attract only "males" and shouldn't expect them to act like men. If you only entertain the worm, then a "worm" is what you end up with. A "woman" who really wants to be with a "man" must demand that he operate as a "man" while presenting herself as a "woman."

From an historical perspective, the mindset of the "male" is very similar to the thinking of the "slave." The mentality of the male is the mentality of the slave. Look at the slave: he's dependent, he's passive, and he completely expects his biological needs to be taken care of by his "master." The "male" brags that he is being used as a stud while someone else has responsibility for his offspring. He values himself as he is valued by those who he depends upon, who value him as a stud. It is important to understand that those who developed and perfected the slave-making process understood some of the basic laws of human nature. They knew the transformational processes that made them into men and how to disrupt those processes in the "males" that they wanted to own as property and did not want to compete with as men. They systematically locked the slaves into "maleness" so that they would remain dependent, non-rebellious and essentially passive in vital areas of human activity. This protected the slave master and kept the slave passive and convinced to accept his status. The "male" mentality predominates in people who are not willing to take the prerogatives and responsibilities of real "men."

Coming into Boyhood

The next step in the transformational process from a "Male" to a "Man" is the development of the "Boy." What is it that moves the Male to becoming a "Boy?" The major force for this change is determined by the development of discipline. It is discipline that transforms passion into a fuel reserve for the self-determination and self-regulation that advances the male into boyhood. The force that begins to control the dependent, passive, passion-driven creature into a being of greater deliberation and more advanced human expression is the restraint and guidance that is obtained by the development of discipline.

The challenge of boyhood is to cultivate a system of self-discipline, but it begins initially from the outside of the self and moves to the inside. The beginning "cocoon" of discipline that advances the rather untamed male towards boyhood is by the force of a caretaker saying to the "male": "No, no, don't do that!" Eventually as the development or growth proceeds, the voice inside of yourself begins to say: "This, I am not going to do." The other side of that inner voice recognizes: "This I will do." As the male weaves a cocoon of selective behaviors around itself, it gradually transforms into a boy. As the voice of discipline exerts its control from the outside direction to the inside, the male begins to transfer its power to the boy as he learns to restrain the demanding urges within to permit the boy to grow. The restraining power of the cocoon of "discipline" lets the male gradually learn the benefits of following the example of the caretaker on whom he depends to demonstrate the power of saying to his maleness: "Wait and be still." The glue of dependency that is abundant during the period of male development now becomes the glue that seals the cocoon for the transformation into even greater power and effectiveness.

"Reasoning" begins to emerge as a part of the cocoon of transformation as the male learns the connections between cause and effect. The panic of being overwhelmed by appetites is gradually reduced with the systematic satisfaction of the needs by the caretaker. Systematic care of his needs without overindulgence or excessive deprivation lets the male learn the safety of survival that alternates from desire to satisfaction. This lesson of cause and effect is the fundamental principle of reasoning that becomes a basic lesson in the fundamentals of reasoning. The "male" going through repeated exercises of this process, learns that delay is tolerable because of a predictable world that does not trigger panic when need is aroused. The experience of an orderly and a predictable world lays the foundation for the fundamentals of reasoning that will permit the growth of rationality. The male learns that things that have happened can and do happen again. As he develops confidence in this order, he can gradually begin to grow the inner voice that says "wait" or "don't do that". These are the building blocks of the critical cocoon of discipline that permits transformation to boyhood. The male must experience order and stillness in his outer world so that he can begin to learn the patience that permits him to learn how to "sit it out and wait to see what happens." Patience, order and repetition become the fundamentals of gaining knowledge and knowledge expands his capacity for weaving the cocoon of rational discipline.

Learning the lessons of reasoning only strengthens the discipline for transformation from maleness to boyhood. Growth into boyhood takes a long time and it still does not assure us of becoming the "Man" (butterfly) we seek to become. The beginning of boyhood is still primarily under the influence of the "male mentality". The state of the early boy mentality represents movement from infancy to a toddler. The newly developed tools of reasoning with the budding of discipline and expansion of knowledge are only additional tools in the arsenal of essentially satisfying the male's mind. Rather than mature objective reasoning, we will have to characterize the early reasoning of the boy's mind with the capacity to be "slick," or manipulative. The boy does not have genuine respect for order, except to the degree that the lessons of order help him to get what he wants. The boy does not yet have respect for order, but he realizes that order serves his purpose. So, this little boy is nice and reasonable so long as Mommy or Daddy is around, but as soon as they turn their backs, he sticks his hand in the cookie jar— at the urging of the "male" that still has primary influence over him. So, the beginning of discipline is there but for the boy mentality, it's an instrument of manipulation rather than fully developed self-navigation. We might call this a form of "slick rationale" rather than truly rational functioning in a more advanced stage. The objective of this "slick rationale" shows a basic grasp of reasoning and order, but only to get what the boy wants with minimal repercussions of deprivation or hurt.

Another quality that begins to emerge in the "boy" stage is the early development of some "sentiment" because of its connection with dependency in the male stage. The boy does not want to really hurt the object that satisfies his needs so long as they are taking care of his desires. He begins to develop some attachment to his caregivers because of the male's continued preoccupation with looking out for himself. How does this work for the boy? He begins to use his attachments with other people as a type of game. Boys like to play games because they have not yet formed a "real" connection to the world around him. The boy is still experiencing the world through the dependent, self-gratification of the male mentality. He plays games with other people and he plays games with himself. Games are played with toys that don't have a reality outside of what he chooses to make them in the service of his own needs and gratification. Games and toys are not about a serious commitment to changing the world, but simply manipulating it with a form of make believe power and symbolic authority. Playing games are not the same as "work" because working requires a more serious commitment to a world larger than the male's little world of self-gratification. Playing games with toys is appropriate for the boy in the cocoon of transformation because they introduce him to the real world of work that changes the world in fundamental ways. There are many examples of the boyish mind in the cocoon of transition from maleness to manhood. Boys like to make jokes and play at reality for his gratification and entertainment. He likes to pretend to be deeply and passionately involved when he is "just playing." Boys who are still in this mind set when they have reached later years reveal the persistence of this mentality with the language they use to describe themselves and their activities. They call themselves "playas" or "playboys" with considerable pride but reveal that they are still dealing with life as a game. Boys have a "game" for everybody when they are not seriously in the reality of life. The cocoon stage is an appropriate stage in the development towards manhood because it provides an extended rehearsal for the realities of life ahead. The cocoon for the boy of boyish age is a necessary rehearsal for the realities of later becoming a "man."

The gang activity is an extension of the rehearsal that many boys go through during this stage because they are in preparation for serious cooperative working relationships. But the gang is only a game with no real resources and still no understanding of the consequences of these pretend actions. He plays with the gang and "hangs-out" with the gang because they are all boys engaged in a game preparing them for the reality of life. The boys haven't yet developed a capacity for meaningful relationships because in the cocoon stage, they are still under the influence of the immature perception of relationships as an extension of the dependency from the "male's mentality". Unfortunately, many times the gangs begin to play with deadly toys like guns, destructive substances and make-believe territories and uniforms and end-up losing their lives or facing some disabling consequences like prison or some other dreaded outcome. The protection of the cocoon permits the boy to play the game with the gang and enjoy the fun, in a secure preparation for the real game of life. While in the protective cocoon, there are those whose more developed eyes can strengthen the discipline that is only gradually beginning to evolve.

Just as we discussed earlier in this section, there is a right time to have the mind of a "male". It is as natural in the growth process as it is to be a caterpillar before becoming a butterfly. When the caterpillar has completed the growth of that stage, it is natural and appropriate for it to surround itself in a cocoon in order to continue the developmental process towards becoming a completed butterfly. Following the same example that we discussed earlier, it is similarly just as natural and correct for the male to transition into a boy. Boyhood is like a cocoon for growth and transformation towards the ultimate objective of becoming a man. All of the characteristics of a boyish mind that we have discussed are appropriate for "boys" while they are in that stage of growth. The difficulty arises when the appropriate time has passed and you still have a boy's mind when it's time to become transformed into a Man. These become the adult bodies occupied by the minds of boys. It is as strange as it would be to see a cocoon with legs, still crawling like a worm and eating leaves like a caterpillar when even the form that it has taken is not equipped for this kind of activity. The cocoon has no legs as the caterpillar did; it doesn't even have a mouth to consume the leaves of its earlier form. The picture of a man's body engaged in boyish activities is just as strange to see. The image of adult male bodies that always have a "game" and spend all of their time playing or even watching games, dressed like boys playing games is just as bizarre a picture. These adults with the boyish minds are pre-occupied with toys (such as an adult with a wife and children who throws away the family income on a flashy two-seater family car that will hardly accommodate two adults.) The "adult boys" will have the largest flat-screen television available with a sound system with the latest variation of quadraphonic sound systems while he has no money to buy his children's school supplies, or even a place in their house for the children to study. The flashy car that's owned by the adult with a boy's mind is like a little boy on his bicycle who rides up to the Little Girl and says: "How do you like my new bike; would you like to go for a ride?" You often see these adult boys with their "pimped out" rides, blasting with their deafening speakers booming in the trunk of their cars, laid so far back in the seat that their heads can't be seen through the tinted windows,30- 40 inch rims that continue to spin when they stop at a traffic light." They are obviously showing off their latest toy as a means of getting attention, just like the "boyish mind" would dictate in this clearly adult body. If they are fortunate enough to maneuver sufficient rent to occupy an apartment, this becomes an equally impractical living environment filled with stuffed cushions, decorated with novelty lights, with every indication that it's a play house or a "playa's pad" rather than a habitat for humanity. The objection to these cartoon like characters is that these are often adults of thirty-five, forty-five, even fifty years old with their children and other responsibilities being taken care of by their "babies' mommas," their mommas or other adults who have chosen to grow up and move beyond being boys or girls. These adult boys spend with the extravagance of children at a carnival and usually earn with minimal initiative. Their preoccupation is trying to impress the "gang" that remains at the same level of their boyhood. They have the latest fashions, the most recent prominent ball player's sneakers and are obviously much more committed to dressing down rather than dressing their minds or building their future. In typical "boyish mentality" selfishness, regardless of what responsibilities they may have to insure their survival and the advancement of their children and communities, they are interested only in themselves for the moment and the current game.

A demonstrated preference for "playing games" as we described above is another example of the "boyish mentality". As we have described above, game-playing is a necessary strategy by which boys learn the process of reasoning that leads to rationality which is a valuable resource for gaining self-discipline. However, an example of a boy who is arrested in his development is when you encounter someone who has paid more money for his entertainment center than he has paid for the books on his shelf or his access to knowledge. A boy has more party space in his place of residence than he has work space. A boy spends more for his liquor than he does for his food. When your view of the opposite sex is exclusively as a potential partner to satisfy your needs for gratification rather than as a companion, then you are still a boy. When your evaluation of relationships with other people are preoccupied with someone to "get back at," "get over on," "get from," or "party with" then you can be rather certain that you are a boy. When the primary use of your reasoning is for the purpose of scheming, lying, gaming or playing then you are stuck in the boy's mentality without the protection of a cocoon.

There certainly is nothing wrong with a game once in awhile as a means of disengaging or "re-creation." In fact, this is a valuable gift that we are able to take into manhood in order to more effectively diversify our energy and emotions, but when the games and the playing become a substitute for determining some strategic life plan, then, you are stuck as a boy. When other men in the world are laying plans to rule the world and you are playing a game of ball, a video game or a card game, then this boyish characteristic is a handicap. When other people are writing books or searching for solutions to the problems of human survival and you are shooting pool or "hoops" then the game is a weapon against your progress and the progress of your community. When your major interest is in the football scores and other people are counting advertising profits, then you are a boy in a man's world or a "slave" on someone's plantation. When you spend six hours of leisure time on the basketball court and thirty minutes or no time in the library or the laboratory, then the game has become a fun road to suicide or sustained captivity. When a community has an excessive number of "boys masquerading as men" (as we will discuss further along in another chapter of this discussion), the result is a community deprived of effective leadership to change the conditions of their people. Until we stop playing games and start dealing with the imperatives of being in an adult world, we will remain as a community in serious trouble.

Even though these principles of manhood development are true for all human communities, this particular discussion is focusing on the relevance of these ideas as we form a Vision for Black Men. The examples that we are using are based on issues that are too common in the African American Community at this particular time in history. Many of the problems that we face in our communities can be understood as a manifestation of this epidemic of "Men" acting like "Boys." The terrible Black-on-Black homicide rates in so many of our cities, gang killings, and so many crimes against each other are clearly examples of boys playing at the game of life. The neglect of too many Black children by their fathers has led to a plague of "Man-Absence" in our communities, because these boys are somewhere playing (or restrained by "Men" who are clear about their Vision of the world and life,) rather than taking care of their manly responsibilities. The drug epidemic that continues to infect our communities is the boyish yearning for a dream world rather than facing the serious matters of reality. It is not accidental that nearly 150 years after legalized slavery in America was ended, one of the supreme insults from the former "slave masters" in referring to "Black Men" is to call us "boys." That insult has even more meaning when you realize that the economic and social conditions in this society have conspired to keep us in the condition of boys, while systematically creating images and circumstances that reward us for our boyish conduct. We are rewarded for playing games, acting like boys seeking entertainment rather than being encouraged and cultivated as real "Men." To be called a "boy" by a "White Man" is the ultimate declaration of victory over our minds. An even greater insult is for that label of "boy" to be accurate, and our conduct validates it with our preoccupation with toys, games and boyish things rather than the real activities of "Men" that we will describe below.

There is considerable evidence to suggest that our retarded growth as boys has been strategically planned by historical deprivations and systematic discrimination as a result of our oppressed state in the Western World. We must ultimately take responsibility for our own growth and development. We do have a choice at this point in history to give up our boyish conduct and adopt a path to real "Manhood." This discussion is intended to help us to first of all, recognize our confusion about the definition of manhood and understand that what we are referring to as being a "man" is actually no more than being "males in the crib" or "boys at play." Too often we don't even have a meaningful idea or vision of what it really means to be a "Man."

Our descriptions, so far, present a rather negative image of the "Boy mentality." It's important to keep in mind that those descriptions only refer to the "Boy" when he should have developed beyond that stage and is still stuck in the cocoon of that period of development. The "Boy" has definitely achieved a level of emancipation beyond the "Male." This level of emancipation puts him in a position to make some independent decisions for himself that the "male" cannot make. The "Boy" doesn't have to go to the bathroom on himself and wait for someone to come and change his diapers. They are not at the complete mercy of the immediate demands of the appetites which is a limitation of the "Male." They are actually physically capable adults who have not acquired the independence of the "Boy" in their mentality and are still acting and thinking like babies when it comes to taking care of themselves and almost incapable of regulating their conduct. Even though these "men" may have reached the age to appear as adults, they are actually males who have not arrived at boyhood in their thinking. Prior to our captivity as slaves, African communities had systematic ways to cultivate the growth of males into boys and ultimately boys into men by systematic "rituals of passage." There were institutionalized practices to advance the "Male" into "Boyhood" and then the "Boy" was trained to develop himself into a "Man." They provided the social systems to advance the males from the dependency of being "Males and "cocoons of practices" to move the "Boys" into manhood. There were practices of instruction and direction that corresponded with the child's maturation that assured that he would make the passage. There was no confusion of indulgent caretakers who created or encouraged various fads and fashions of child-rearing that led to boys being stuck as males and then remaining "boys" rather than becoming Men. The community took responsibility to advance the transformation of these people to become the men that they should be, just as nature insures the evolution of the caterpillar to enter the cocoon and become butterflies.

Transformation from Boy to Man

How do we get from being a "Boy" to becoming a "Man"? As we have already discussed, the key quality of the cocoon that transforms us from a Male to a Boy is the substance of discipline that frees the Boy from being a slave of the Male mentality. Discipline or learning to exercise control over the self is the transformative energy in the cocoon of boyhood. The energy that begins to break the cocoon and transform the boy into manhood is Knowledge. The reasoning gained from discipline should begin to grow into rationality, permitting the boy to gradually expand his consciousness. As we have discussed above, the boy should be guided in the use of immature reasoning so that it develops into rational understanding and meaningful choices. If the boy stays at this level of simple cause and effect reasoning for selfish gratification, he can become entrapped in the form of the boyish mentality. Such entrapment results in matured bodies, looking like men, which are still thinking and acting with the minds of boys. This is why fathers, teachers, uncles, brothers and other role models are so important. The influences of these models who have successfully navigated passage out of the cocoon of boyhood are the instruments of guidance that help boys move towards manhood. Too many of our young men get stuck in this boyish stage of development because they are improperly guided and end up being taken away to prison or even worse, the cemetery. Rationality and the growth of consciousness is a natural possibility or potential, but unlike the cocooned caterpillar, it must be tended and guided in order for it to develop properly.

What is Consciousness? Consciousness is awareness. What is Awareness? Awareness is the ability to see accurately what really is. Not, what one wants or dreams the world to be based upon his wants, needs and demands, but an accurate picture of where you stand in space, time and in relationship to other human beings. This means that it is critical to have a realistic picture of oneself and the world in which he finds himself. How does the Boy gain this information in order to be transformed into a "Real Man?" The most effective way to gain proper orientation is to be thrown into the center of the arena of life with the watchful and protective eye of those who have moved into this stage. To be sheltered, indulged, spoiled, enabled and made to believe that the world owes you something and requires nothing of you is deadly for proper growth. The boy learns about himself from the confrontation of problems and being forced to find solutions for those problems. As you overcome your fears and face the real problems within the level of your capability, you are forced to "sink or swim." If you begin to sink the protective model is there to rescue you, even though you may fail to graduate from that stage at that time, you are saved from drowning. If you swim, then you have graduated in your first step on towards becoming a real "Man".

This simply means that the process of educating our boys is carefully determining their capability and requiring them to tackle real life problems and watch them find solutions. They should have early work responsibilities, management responsibilities, and social responsibilities. If they don't put up their toys, then when they are ready to play with them again, they won't be able to find them. As they advance into boyhood, work must precede play and without work there is no time to play. If they are not careful of the needs of those weaker than they are, then, they don't get the respect of those who are stronger. Rewards should follow some form of accomplishment and not simply desiring things to magically make them come to you. These responsibilities force the muscles of manly growth to develop. As the boy increasingly masters levels of responsibilities, he discovers the vastness of his potential and then moves to ever-increasing higher horizons. If his energies are only directed towards fun and games, jokes and play, then he continues to recycle in that limited dimension and his growth becomes stifled.

The wings of manhood begin to expand as the boy is able to exercise them. If boys are permitted to do a little then they receive a little. The ultimate emergence into manhood requires man-ly responsibilities and commitments. For example the graduation from boyhood to manhood is reflected by the willingness to make a commitment to a relationship. The achievement of manhood means that one gives up being a "playa" and jumps into the water of marriage. You can't claim to be a man if you are satisfied with just "shacking" because this is just a game and you are not required to take full responsibility for your actions. We learn our true poten-tial when we are forced to take full responsibility for our actions and the consequences of those actions. "Shacking" does not take full responsibility for the relationship and the other person you are committing to, because it keeps an escape door open. Marriage is escapable but not without a thorough lesson in commitment, deci-sions, actions and consequences which are the wings of manhood. Even in a failed marriage, the lessons are irreversible and advance you into manhood. "Shacking" lets you play the game of commit-ment and being a husband without the certain lessons that come with the actual action. The avoidance of marriage and the choice to "play" husband keeps you in the mentality of "boys" who "play house" and not build homes.

A man must understand that his decisions are binding and there is real significance to real decisions with real consequences. (Remember: learning reality is what transforms the reasoning of the boy to the rationality that makes the man.) The kind of responsibil-ity that one assumes in marrying into a relationship grows an impor-tant wing (or muscle) into your manhood. This kind of commit-ment is so important to manhood development that marriage is an accepted process almost universally. You will never learn the role of "husbanding" until you decide to be a husband, not a roommate, but a committed partner. You have got to know what it means be with this other person (for better or for worse) and not be able to get away by simply packing your bags and moving out. There is instruc-tive pressure that comes from being bound and responsible to and for another person socially, economically, legally, spiritually and psychologically. The legal paper of matrimony is not the key to helping you progress into "Manhood", the key is learning the responsibility that goes with commitment. It is the commitment that cultivates the man potential in you and expands the reach of the boy's wings and develops the "Man" muscle. The responsibilities of being a husband bring down the rain to the soil of your being to enable you to handle the droughts and the floods of the real world. When you take on the lessons of being a husband, you stimulate your growth from a boy to a man by the expansion of your consciousness from just "I" to "We". You begin to discover muscles that you didn't know that you had and to understand that you can share yourself and not simply be concerned about yourself. Unlike the boy, you recognize that "We" is actually a larger self than just "I". This expansion of your sentiments to include more than just "Me," helps to break away the cocoon and release the fully developing "Man." Let's be very clear that we are not simply referring to the romantic ceremonies with rings, jumping brooms, costly costumes and honeymoons or even the legal document of a marriage license. The critical lesson is not ceremonial, but the transformative mental capacity to be sincerely committed to another human being.

After you have accepted the lessons of responsibility for the "We" in the training camp of marriage, a new urge begins to grow in the developing consciousness of the Man. This more advanced level of transformation is the urge for "Fathering." The "male" and the "boy" experience the fleeting pleasure of the sexual and romantic moment, but the growth of the "Man" expands that "moment" into a sustained permanence of joy. The urge to become a father is the longing to transcend even the limitations of time. In order for this ultimate expression of your "Manhood" to come to fruition, there is an even higher challenge to the muscles of your possibility. This urge actually represents a desire to further expand the "We" of the marriage to an "Us" of a family. You must now come to add-on the responsibility that has grown from a single "self" to a couple into the awesome challenges of an even larger expansion of your "self" as multiple. There are some real challenges that you must encounter for this graduation: For example, you must accept the responsibility of care and nurturance for the "We" to expand to include not only a partner in development, but now in the Us, there is a helpless person for whom you must have responsibility. This multiplies the weights for the muscle development of Manhood. You might have worked from early morning to early evening with the predictable exhaustion of such a day and then as soon as you are comfortably relaxing in the "I" in bed for some much needed rest, this helpless child yells out demanding attention from the responsible caretakers. Even if these duties are shared by the "We", they are never fully delegated because the initiate into Fatherhood has to respond to the dependent's demand. Despite the fact that you might ache from exhaustion, you are being taught the lessons of responsibility for those who cannot be responsible for themselves, which is the early passage into the growth of "Father." When the doctor diagnoses that the new-comer has an ear infection, you begin to literally understand that you have grown another set of ears and the pain in those little ears are now your pain. The developing Man must make his toys secondary because he has to keep milk in the refrigerator before he puts gas in his "ride"; he must also buy toys to entertain the baby and decrease his budget for his own "toys." It is through this experience as a father that you are introduced to an expanded sense of time and can begin to know the transcendent time that a "boy" can never even imagine. With the expanded vision of your child's eyes, you can today glimpse into a tomorrow that the "I" is not likely to see. You can peep across time into a future through those little eyes that you have fathered. As you participate and insure the development of your child, the Father can soar into and contribute to a time that is not yet born. This is the reward for the sacrifice that is made in caring and cultivating the challenges of being "Father" because you make a mark on a time that the "I" will never directly experience. You actually have the opportunity to create your own immortality through the building of being a Father. This is why the image of the butterfly that flies from the cocoon takes on very graphic meaning as we contemplate the process of being transformed from Boys to Men.

These living examples of family development become concrete illustrations of the process of the expansion of consciousness. The growth and transformation from family development are simple pictures and rather universal in their occurrence, but the same consequence emerges from the application of one's self seriously to the problems of life. Not everyone in the human family is privileged to become a "Father" to their biological offspring. You may become a teacher, an artist, a scientist, a healer, an advocate, a businessman or a musician, but the model of serious application of one's energies to the challenges of developing new ideas and creations has the same transformative effect as "Fathering" ones biological or adopted child. Boys are transformed into Men through the same dedication and serious commitment to something larger than himself. The process transforms the boy into a man. As you apply yourself to confronting the real challenges of life and realize that these challenges build the muscles of your manhood and expand your consciousness, you move from the limited and restricted stage in the cocoon of boyhood. The same lessons that the husband and father learns about commitment and responsibility are necessary devices to break open the cocoon of boyhood and transform you into manhood. The discipline that moved you from Maleness to Boyhood must be expanded; the mastery from reasoning to rationality must be cultivated and the living process of breaking down the selfish boundaries of the "I" from your individual needs and wants metaphysically transform a Boy into a Man.

This growth into manhood builds our muscle for leadership. You gradually learn to lead increasingly large communities as you master leadership of smaller communities. Discipline is the tool to give you leadership over your smallest "community of self" as a boy and a larger community as a husband moving into manhood. Then you expand your leadership capacity as you grow into effective fatherhood or worker, or student, etc. You must first become a king in the personal kingdom that is situated on your feet before you can become a king in a "relationship kingdom," and eventually in the bigger kingdom of the family or the business or some other creative venture that you have decided to "father." Each step in the process prepares you for expanded capacity. The idea is that Manhood is a process and not an automatic event that comes like the change in your shoe size.

As we have mentioned above in this discussion, African American men have been strategically taken out of our minds and confined in this insane mind of a boy or either just a male. This mentality of immature development in adult bodies served and maintains our captivity in slavery. The mind of a man revolts against being a slave, whereas a "male" or a "boy" is easily controlled and held captive without chains, even. The consciousness of a "man" equips one to seek the highest form of human freedom and is not satisfied even with the limitations of "emancipation." This is an important distinction because we are aware that emancipation limits your independence and often results in a subtle form of hidden slavery. Emancipated slaves found themselves returning to their former masters in search of the fundamentals for survival because they had not been able to fully develop as liberated "men." Even several generations later, we have former enslaved Africans with the minds of "boys" who are incapable of establishing independent thought and action and self-determined leadership. The emancipated boy's mind prefers the master's reality to the establishment of his own reality. Boys keep returning to the confines of the intellectual, economic or even social plantation because they have not fully developed to become the self-determined men that we have described in our description of the development of the man's mind that has expanded to engage in the type of responsibility that men who are free and fully developed manifest. Emancipated boys are basically materialistic and dependent on their toys as we have described earlier. As we described above boys define their adequacy and their power by the toys or materials that they are able to acquire. When possible they remain confined in a boy's world on the plantation of debt and dependency. These emancipated boys are manipulated by the constant change in fashions, designer sneakers or other plantation toys. In fact these contemporary "emancipated boys" are kept on the plantation by a fashion or entertainment industry that keeps them chasing materials, games, outfits or toys that create the illusion of freedom and power that characterizes "boys" in our discussion above. Some of our most intellectually gifted "boys" who have not become "men" will not entertain independent ideas that are not legitimized by the masters who have gained independence for themselves because they have evolved into the true Man's mind that carries the responsibilities that have transformed them into self-determined agents through the mastery of self-knowledge.

The emancipated boy who has not grown into the manhood through the transformation of his appropriate cocoon has some major human restrictions and handicaps in his leadership skills. He is certainly much better off than the "male slave" who is in absolute captivity. We can perhaps describe the emancipated boy as a "servant" rather than a slave. The difference is that the servant is one who receives some compensation and even recognition for his dependency and he is not serving against his will as the male slave. But neither the servant nor the slave belongs to himself because they are owned and directed by the influence of men who know who they are and what their human responsibility requires. The boy is economically a servant because he has nothing of genuine significance that can change the course of social and human events. Boys seldom consider developing independent resources or even sharing those resources with other boys who share their social condition. The emancipated boy is conditioned to take his entire resources home to "Daddy," because of his mental dependency. Boys have to take their resources back to their caretaker because they have not established an independent mind set to use them to build for themselves. Even the mental goods and creative ideas of the emancipated "boys" must depend on their evolved "men" benefactors in order to obtain their recognition.

Men who have been naturally and properly transformed and developed a Vision of who they are consistent with the pattern we have described in this discussion acquire a higher consciousness. When we come into this higher consciousness, we are able to relate to Men as "Fellow-men". We are not prone to play boyish games of trying to prove that we are more "manly" than other Men as in a competitive sport. Such men are able to relate to Women who have acquired their "Womanhood", not as trophies or objects but with respect and in partnerships. These fully developed men who know themselves in their true identity are not prone to the disastrous divisions that have been historically destructive to our "Emancipated slave Communities." Some of our very gifted African American leadership could have made so much more progress if we had not been entrapped in "Emancipation Games." For example we would be so much better off if Dr. W.E.B. DuBois, Marcus Garvey and Booker T. Washington had been able to see the similarity in their Visions for African American people and work with each other as "Fellow-men" rather than competitive "boys." Pan Africanism championed by Dr. DuBois was not so different from the "Back to Africa" vision of Marcus Garvey or the "self-determination" philosophy of Booker T. Washington. Just suppose that The Honorable Elijah Muhammad and Dr. Martin Luther King, Jr. could have gotten beyond the surface differences that separated them and could have united their visions for the "Freedom" rather than "emancipation" of African American people. Suppose that Mr. Muhammad and Dr. King could have sat down together as "Fellowmen "and Mr. Muhammad said: "Let's do something for ourselves" and Dr. King might have replied: "We shall overcome!" They could have joined hands as Men who knew who they were and transformed Chicago, Atlanta and the entirety of the United States of America. Our communities are deficient today because these great and powerful minds could not get together because of left-overs of incomplete development from the plantation trauma.

The disabling partisanship that has characterized the conduct of American politics in recent years demonstrates that Leaders who have failed to acquire full manhood engage in similar boyish games that can actually paralyze even a powerful nation such as the United States of America. Effective leaders must be evolved in their development as Men (and Women) in order to interact for the good of the constituency that they represent. Without the achievement of the kind of evolved development that we are describing in this discussion, leaders become ineffective at the Community level, the State level or even the National level resulting in deficiency for the entire society. Anyone who claims to be an effective and deserving leader must be freed from the cocoon of boyhood in order to qualify for such a level of responsibility. The person who is a leader must have the consciousness to see problems from a perspective considerably broader than the "male" or "boy" consciousness. Leaders will necessarily have to approach the resolution of problems with a commitment to the much larger "Us" rather than just a small "I". To effectively lead, "Men" must be willing to struggle to find a point of communality despite the contrived differences which appeal to the "Boy" or "Male" consciousness. This requires a willingness to confront themselves to grow out of the "Boyish" cocoon and into a fully developed Man.

The "Man" consciousness naturally develops a strong community interest because they understand that community is only an enlarged "Family." When there is no community interest then there are ghettoes of decay. Irresponsible landlords may neglect their property and refuse to invest in painting the walls, but when "Men" live there, they will insure that the sidewalks are cleaned and they will refuse to let the children draw graffiti on the walls adding to the decay. Community interest will motivate men to improve on whatever they have in order to transform it to what they want. The Man's mind is driven by a sense of responsibility, initiative and transformation. Every "man" has a sense of responsibility for every child, every other adult and every person in that community and ultimately should expand for everyone in the city, state and nation. The "manly mind" does not have to be elected or appointed as the leader; he is naturally inclined with the instincts of the leader. In communities where Men live, there are no robberies, rapes, child abuse and molestation of children, even with no police force around. "Men" can change communities if they have been effectively transformed themselves. Men can develop independent schools, independent businesses, and independent thought and disciplined communities because they have achieved these qualities in themselves. Men can learn the difference between love and romance

and teach the romantic, males, boys, females and girls, the difference by their example.

The "Man" consciousness that is continuously being transformed
grows into a "God" consciousness. No, we are not suggesting that
the man becomes a preacher or "God!" We are suggesting that as
the butterfly leaves its cocoon and soars towards the heavens, the
"Man" consciousness expands his horizons to the highest aspirations
of the human being. This God-consciousness is not a religious concept in the denominational or sectarian sense. "God consciousness"
has little to do with going to a church, mosque, shrine or synagogue.
It's not even about engaging in home-based rituals. Such visits and
practices may heighten our awareness of the God, but they don't
necessarily transform us into the image of God. This transformation
of consciousness and awareness permits us to live the process of
the Creator that planted a seed in the essence our being to evolve
us into a higher form of life. This Divine Order moves the Earth at a
consistent speed transforming and stimulating growth in the very
process of its movement. This Divine Order maintains a consistent
form and pattern, changing the seasons; bringing life from death
and death into life; this Plan changes the winds, directs the tides,
schedules the eruptions of volcanoes, stirring storms systematically
and alters the form of the earth at the point of its flaws with geo-
logical quaking that rearrange the crust of the earth. This creative
force is laid down in the structure of processes of life, growth and
transformation. The human being is a part of that Infinite inscruta-
ble Plan. This Creative Force that programmed the analog for all of
these processes of Nature is also capable of designing our minds so
that it might manifest according to its intended order. There is no
doubt that we can achieve whatever is defined in our nature as our
potential. The key to unlock this potential is knowledge or awareness of our possibilities. Whatever we can understand, we can be;
whatever we can project in our thinking and our conduct, we can
become. No matter how severe the sabotage of our "Manhood"
might have been, the "Divine Plan" cannot be destroyed and it can
be retrieved. It simply requires us to know what we were supposed
to be and take the responsibility to let be what was intended to be
from the beginning.

Men of the African world were the first to stand-up from the
slump of the beast and become men and it was those Men who gave
the world its first hymn of human liberation and the song of human
freedom. This song of human liberation and transformation must

come from the very soul of the human being, not just an exercise of the mind and body. The Ancient African Ancestors understood the beauty of a liberated soul, which was for the human being, like the wings that freed the butterfly from the gravity of earth. This is why those African people, under whatever conditions, could sing the song of human possibility and resilience. It was this faith in the human potential that fueled human development in civilization, science, religion and human growth. This deep faith in the human possibility and consciousness of a Higher Reality that we have come to refer to as "God" has given African people the power to take even alien concepts of religion and convert them to their own. The European captors came with missions of Christianity and Africans constructed a theology that has the captors "trying to be born again." When the so-called "born again" Christians declare their desire to be re-born, they are expressing the wish to be like the children of Africa. Though we were put into bondage by their distortions of Christianity that the Europeans altered to fit their image of the world, we took the deformity and transformed it and made it do for us what it was not intended to do. The Arabs came with Islam and we took it and built the great civilizations of Continental Africa such as Timbuktu.

The "male" mind is only capable of sight-seeing in the world as reality passes them by. They observe passively with a hand outreached seeking a hand-out. Boys have dreams. They dream and wonder, while living in an unreal world in their minds. Only Men have Visions of what could be and they exercise the initiative to transform the world through collective leadership, work and shared development. If you decide to be who you were intended to be, then the world can be transformed as you were transformed from a passive recipient to an instrument of change.

2

Transcending Images of Black Manhood

There is something very special when we come together as
a group of people. We generate a kind of energy that trans-
mits a special kind of communication, knowledge and understanding. It's a form of transcendence that immediately erases
the distinctions, the disagreements and we become unified as "One"
with each other that there is no psychological theory to explain. We
talk about it in our proverbs when we say: "It takes a village to raise a
child." This "village" is not an individual but a unified whole of multiple
experiences, talents and dreams that gel into this unified parent that
is poured into the development of a child. This power of unification
where we lose ourselves into a larger self that is extremely gifted,
powerful and effective when it is properly understood. I am not talking about a "mob mentality" but something that is very constructive
that we must cultivate and use in a positive way because there is a
hidden, even mystical power in that transcendent unification that is
very important for us to understand and utilize in the building of our
people and humanity as a whole. Every people within their cultural
and historical experiences develop power systems that emerge out
of their definitions of who they are. It is these unique systems of collective power that enables them to be effective in the social, physical, economic and emotional environments that they inhabit. Every
group of people has a responsibility to know who they are in their
uniqueness so that they are able to interact on an equal footing with
other human beings who are drawing from the well of their unique
cultural and historical experiences. It's very similar to what we find

in nature with certain bird or mammal communities that have their special songs, nesting and feeding patterns built from the adaptation and survival in the environment over time that protect them from prey and empower them to be competitive in the ecology of life forms. This special power that is generated from our "collective connectedness" that is somehow related to our effectiveness and resilience as a people. Every people have their special cultural strengths that they put forth a great deal of effort to identify and preserve. There are general human qualities that we share with all humans, but unique and special qualities that make us different from other communities of humans. Some people, for example, celebrate individual heroes that serve as the role models for their excellence. They celebrate the power of the individual who distinguishes himself from the ordinary and they use this power to create their models of greatness. Their society has statues or icons of these distinct individuals that the young are taught to imitate and they use these images to empower their "village" or "tribe". The fact that we recognize that our power comes in this collective form doesn't make us superior or inferior to any other people, it's simply our special power in the competition for life resources. This is the color of our "human feathers."

Relevance of Scriptural Metaphors

As we continue to explore the "Visions for Black Men," it is appropriate that we seek to understand the special identity and unique power systems of Black Men. In the first chapter, we described the developmental process of the Man as he transitions from his beginning of life to the fruition or maturing of manhood. As we discussed in the preceding chapter, there is certain universality to the process but our intention is to understand this process in the context of the unique Black experience which is the reason that we drew upon examples from the historical journey of being African-Americans seeking to know how our development has been influenced by these experiences.

As we were able to find in the previous chapter, from the universal pictures of nature some meaningful ideas about the development of Black Men, we should be able to gain some insight into the unique development of African American Men in the religious stories of human development. The universality of scriptural stories or metaphors should give us some "Transcendent Images" about the development of men in general and the Black Man in particular. These scriptural stories have spoken to the evolution of Men and their struggles over hundreds of years and many different communities of men have found themselves reflected in these images. In one of these Scriptural stories (that is found in the Torah of the Jewish people, the Christian Bible and the Holy Qur'an of the Muslims) we are told that Men were taken captive and lost their natural identity and as a result became the oppressed slaves of Wise Men of great power whose knowledge of themselves was the source of their power. After many generations, the "Wise Captors" began to hear rumors in the land that a Liberator was going to be born to the oppressed people who would provide Leadership of the captives to help them regain their power through restoring knowledge of their original and lost identity. In this story, the Wise Men who understood the spiritual world, were called by the name of "High Priests" were summoned by the King Pharaoh. The High Priests or most knowledgeable Men of the Land came to the Pharaoh and told him that a Liberator was going to come and would remove the veil of ignorance from the captives, teach them their natural identity and they would be relieved from captivity. They said to the Pharaoh: "It is decreed that the people who you hold in bondage will be relieved from their captivity. In time there will be a Leader, a Person, a Mentality to emerge among the Men and it will serve as a liberating force in the Land and the captives will be freed from your physical and political oppression, regardless of what you may try to do to stop them." Pharaoh who had received the legacy of his captives from many generations, said: "How can this be? I am naturally the master and they have been our slaves over many generations and this is the way that things have always been." The Wise Men counseled Pharaoh that the only way that he could preserve his power and maintain this order was to destroy the Promised Liberator by killing all of the Male Children born to the enslaved people so that the "Males" would not develop into a Liberating Man." This story unfolds in such a way that the Liberator manages to avoid the decree of being killed as a male child and grows as a Boy and into a Man in the very house of Pharaoh and became the promised Liberator known as Moses and sure enough, he sets the captives free with the knowledge of their true identity as "Men".

In another story several generations later, there is another lapse in the consciousness of the freed men and they once again become captives of the Men who are able to gain the power of self-knowledge and enslave the ones without such knowledge. The clarity of the knowledge of natural growth and the development of higher consciousness fell into the hands of a captor and was lost to the "Israelites" and they became slaves once again, this time the Wise men were led by a King named "Herod." In this Judeo-Christian story, once again rumblings began to occur in the land that the people of Israel required a Leader/Liberator. The clarity of the lessons of proper growth and development and the path to God-consciousness had once again become corrupted and distorted and there was a need to purify the lessons for the development of liberating Leadership. The Word began to spread around the Land of Herod, that a "Messiah" or Leader was going to emerge from the oppressed people. Again, Herod enacted the same form of "capital punishment" that was initiated by Pharaoh in the earlier story when such a rumor began to circulate. King Herod called in his spiritually Wise Men and said: "How can we stop the birth of this promised "Messiah" or New Leader.?" He wanted to know, "How can we stifle the resurgence of this Message of Truth and maintain the power that we have over these oppressed and powerless people?" Herod demanded to know: "Aren't our armies strong enough?" "Weren't our indoctrinations effective enough; didn't we put enough shackles on their minds that they should never get free? The Wise Men said to Herod, "there is a Force that is working that is more powerful than you are." Herod asked his Wisest Men, "What can I do; how can I then be assured that this new Messiah will not come?" Herod's Wisest Men, went into consultation and returned with the same advice that the Wise Men of Pharaoh had given him, many generations before: "You must kill all the Male children of the oppressed, since you don't know from whence this Savior is coming."So Herod sent out a decree that all of the first born "male" children of the oppressed should be killed," in order to prevent that one of these males might grow to become a Man who was capable of Leadership, and saving the oppressed. (The full recital of these stories can be found in the 28th Sura or chapter of the Muslim, Holy Qur'an and in the 2nd Chapter of the Book of Matthew in the Christian Holy Bible.)

In order to really understand the universal message that is being told in these Religious Scriptures, it is necessary to transcend the mythological images by trying to impose historical fact where the symbolic message is more extensive and inclusive. A part of the strategy of the oppressor is to convince the oppressed that messages of universal significance are the exclusive folk tales of the oppressor and have significance only for them and in their historical development. Scriptural Truth is not something that is time-limited or limited to a particular people but they are transcendent images of human development. No particular people have a monopoly on such universal Truth, even though the captors are strategically determined to convince the captives of this. The only "chosen" people are the "choosing people." If a people choose the path of Truth, they are chosen by the consequences of the chosen path. The natural order demands that when things get out of order, there is an inescapable tendency to move back onto the natural path. An unjustified enslavement, oppression and captivity of a people are out of the natural order. These transcendent images tell us that again and again when this happens, there are going to be some rumblings in the land that a Messiah or a Leadership to restore natural order among the captives is going to grow in intensity. Whoever may be the contemporary Pharaoh, King (Herod) or National President is going to be troubled by this inevitability. These stories tell us that the predictable response of the power-holders will be to do whatever is necessary to disrupt this inevitable growth towards Leadership among the enslaved people or captives. The strategy is predictable that they will try to stop the emergence of the new mind ("Man") by sending out a decree that all the male children must be killed or potential "Men" will be killed as "Males". If we will read these images with a clear mind, we will realize that we have arrived at the time of the symbolic prophecies of what would happen at the time of this confrontation. Even though we may not have documentation of what happened in Egypt when the Pharaoh issued his decree or in the time of when Herod issued his decree, there certainly is considerable evidence of what is happening after 400 years of African captivity in America. Whether we look at the prison statistics, the numbers of Black male children being killed or the intensified efforts to block the emergence of a new Manly leadership, a decree has clearly been issued that the first born Black man child must die, to prevent the change that will come.

Various Definitions of "Death"

When we observe what's happening to Black Males, it is a consequence of the decree that has gone out from the Leadership of Pharaoh or Herod. "Death and dying" is the most consistent image of Black males in America. It's important that we understand that the "Death" spoken of in these stories has a much broader meaning than the physical slaughter of the "first born sons" that is portrayed in the scriptural stories. In part, the image can be seen as literal when we find in contemporary American society that the group with the shortest life expectancy happens to be Black Males, who are most likely to die before the age of twenty and least likely to live until sixty. Black males are the most likely victims of homicide, suicide, police brutality, accidents, drug overdose and other forms of premature death than any other group in modern society. Death and dying is the most likely destiny for Black males whether urban or rural and regardless of economic class. If we combine these fatal statistics with the self-destructive life styles that seem to be programmed into young Black "boys", then we can account for another substantial number of destroyed Black males. Whether it's the mind-paralyzing addiction to drugs, alcohol or tobacco or the worst possible diets leading to premature death, the decree is indisputable. If we follow the scriptural metaphor, we need not be surprised at this deadly and dismal picture because, the "decree" has been sent out that the "first born male child must be killed."

Unfortunately, the transcendent image does not restrict the picture of death to the destruction of the physical life. To be restricted from productive life within the society is a form of social/ economic death. Those Black males who survive physically die mentally and socially in disproportionate numbers in America's prison systems. The majority of creative Black minds who are males are locked up in prisons during the most productive years of their lives. (M.Alexander, 2010). During the years when non-Black males are primarily in universities, colleges and training institutes, gaining the skills that will ensure that they can maintain their power of societal control, African-American future leaders, advocates, educators, directors and scientists are locked away playing dominoes, games and watching "boyish" fantasies on the television screens that are set on standard channels of mental deprivation. This becomes an institutional death that destroys the motivation for self-direction, self-determination and the necessary rationality that prepares you for the achievement of Manhood. Even after release from prison, these males are stigmatized in such a way that even with the desire for productive lives; nearly every arena is closed to them. The stigma of being a "convicted felon" rather certainly continues a life sentence that makes release from the institutional prison very similar to being in a physical prison. Except in very rare occasions this death eliminates them as agents to change the society in a constructive way. The only real alternative is to avoid the death of the institution and for them to defy the system intended to keep them as males by using their incarceration to free their minds and resist becoming imprisoned. Rather than protesting for more "play" time, they should protest for books, educational materials and ways to free their minds, advancing them towards manhood rather than being comfortable as boys. Incarcerated men should begin to use this restricted time as an opportunity to develop "think tanks," and to study. Rather than finding some way to get contraband to get them "high" or spending wasted time with fantasies of the sexual gratification that they miss or some scheme that put them where they are in the first place, they should use that energy to transform themselves. It is rather easy to exchange stories with other prisoners who were just as unsuccessful at crime as you were which is why they are confined just like you; instead they should decide: "We are going to make this a think tank and study how to become real men." We have nothing to do for five, ten or fifteen years, so let's try to get as many books and study materials to help us know who we are and how we got in this situation; let's free our minds, even though our bodies are confined. If this was how prisoners would begin to use their time in study groups and think tanks about effective human development, there is no doubt that the powers that want to see them as "institutionally dead" would begin to release prisoners on a wholesale basis. If they found that this form of "death" was not working, there would be a radical change in the prison system. Wardens, judges and correctional experts would begin to decree: "Get out of here; we don't want you in jail." "Go back into the streets and find you a needle, some dope or alcohol and self-destruct by whatever means you want." "We don't want you in here using our resources to transform yourself from "boys" to "men." As long as you accept the role of being a prisoner and act like a prisoner by accepting their definition of a prisoner, they will keep you as prisoners. Pharaoh, Herod and his Wise Men don't want real "Men" in prison particularly working together in a constructive way rather than trying to destroy each other like savage boys. The huge prison system in America which is the largest in the world and filled with Black Men is a form of death. It is a modern institutionalized way to "kill off the young male children." They could just as easily become the largest educational system in the world if the incarcerated would devote every spare moment to self-improvement and self-knowledge. By flipping this script, Black Men would begin to emerge from prisons rather than Black Boys and in the not too distant future the forces that profit by stifling Black Man development would close those institutions down and seek an alternative strategy to stop true Manhood development.

The very high and disproportionate rate of unemployment of Black Men is not an accident caused by them. Inactivity and dependency stagnates and eventually destroys the human mind. Another way to block the growth of "Men" is to make it impossible or extremely difficult for them to operate as economic agents within a society. When men are forced into situations where they cannot control their lives and unable to provide support and direction for their families or to build and secure institutions for the growth of their communities, their very human nature revolts! When the opportunity to obtain resources for life is blocked, there is a revolt of human despair in response to the dependency and helplessness that leads to social and economic death.

Of course, the most promising young minds are "killed" by systematically turning them against themselves with a miseducational process that fails to give them a valid knowledge and respect for who they are. These young, brilliant but misinformed minds should be the conscious and committed leadership of their communities. Instead, they have been "killed" and have become alienated from their own communities and from themselves. They are "mentally dead," desiring any and everything that doesn't look like them: they want a non-Black woman for a mate, a job that brings no resources to the African American community; they want to live in non-Black communities, drive cars that return no resources to their own communities and want to be identified with anything or anybody unlike themselves. This is the most deceptive form of "mental death" because they appear to be alive despite being completely dead as productive agents to transform their environments. They are actually "zombies" or "ghosts" held up as examples of achievement in a society that has no interest in seeing them transformed into true and effective leaders. Whether they are sports heroes, entertainers or successful achievers in the realm of "miseducation", they are projected as desirable role models by those with no commitment to genuine Black Men operating in their people's self-interest. In many ways, they are worst than those Black men who are in the cemetery because there is no doubt about the terminated life of the ones in the graves. The ones in the cemetery know that they are dead and any living people know they are dead, but these miseducated and misdirected "mentally dead" have learned to confuse life with death and present the impression to others and to themselves that they are alive. These "mentally dead" are a very serious problem because they don't realize that their skills are useless if they are not first of all, in the service of their people and the development of their communities. This is the successful work of Pharaoh (Herod) and his agents who has identified them by scouting skilled high school athletes and saying to these young males with the greatest mental potential: "You really don't want to go to one of those 'inferior' predominantly Black schools; come on over here with us at one of these predominantly White universities; we will give you a fully paid scholarship." "Do you want to be a Physicist or a Lawyer? We've got some minority development programs for your people just like you and you won't have to take any of that Black History Stuff; you won't have to see any professors that look anything like you; we will assure you of the 'best' education in the world."

There is a systematic strategy of ensuring that African-American students are limited in their exposure to the unique needs of their people, the special knowledge that stimulates their identity and few role models that could inspire them to develop a commitment of service, these potential leaders are never born. At the end of two, four, eight or ten years of this kind of selective "miseducation" our potential leaders are completely impotent and dead. Such students leave these Institutions with multiple and impressive degrees in every imaginable field of study but they are of no benefit to their communities that desperately need them. They are identified as the qualified leaders for the oppressed communities from which they have come and are even viewed by the members of those communities as their appropriate leadership, their brightest thinkers, and their young scholars but they are not "theirs." Instead they are actually Pharaoh's "scholars." A further illustration of this betrayal of "dead leadership" can be seen in the limited presence of young scholars in those professional organizations that have historically addressed the special needs of their communities. Organizations such as the National Barristers' Association (Black Lawyers), National Medical Association (Black Doctors), National Dental Association (Dentists), and the National Association of Black Psychologists are all suffering to remain solvent while the new young scholars cannot wait to join the Professional Organizations committed to the growth and empowerment of non-Black people. After these historical Black Organizations were decreed as "no longer necessary" following the civil rights struggles of the latter half of the last century, the generation that was cultivated with an alien set of priorities only wants membership in the predominantly White Professional Organizations. They no longer understand that there are unique needs that the oppressed communities of previous generations still have the kind of relevance that led to the formation of these ethnically-oriented professional organizations. They believe that these Black Professional Organizations were simply formed because they were not permitted in White Professional Organizations. They don't realize that there was recognition of some special issues that needed special attention from Professionals who were committed to being effective leaders for their communities. They want to be with Pharaoh's scholars and His wise men that are primarily committed to the effective management of Pharaoh's kingdom and maintaining his power. A part of that alien kingdom's commitment is still the fulfillment of the decree: that the "young male children" should be killed in order to avoid the coming of a liberating "Messiah" for the oppressed.

Moses and Jesus in "Egypt"

Pharaoh (Herod's) decree that "all the young male children should be killed" is a vital part of the plot (agenda) of these stories which is why it occurs in both of these "scriptural images." This death, whether mentally, physically, socially, institutionally or economically must be seen as a necessary component of the stories. In both stories, Pharaoh or Herod, with his superior power in the material world was very successful in executing this decree. The stories tell us that the Kings of Power were very successful in killing many thousands of young children in order to stop the birth of the Prophesied Leader of the oppressed. If we take these images from the scriptures and place them in contemporary settings, we are able to see the young males' blood flowing in the streets of Chicago, New York, St. Louis, Cleveland, Los Angeles and all over America. The "transcendent images" must be understood as everything from violence against black life from cops, gangs, the lack of education, drug abuse and all of the other forms of death that we have described above. Despite the evidenced of success of the "Kings" in achieving their objective, they forgot that there was a Higher Order that had laid a plan and even though Pharaoh or Herod seemed to be successful, the Higher Order was destined to win.

Pharaoh got excellent advice from his Wise Spiritual Advisors and did all that he could to disrupt the plan, but the Liberator managed to be hidden in his very own house. The Liberator that was prophesied to come wasn't in the streets where the killing was taking place but safely protected in Pharaoh's house eating his food and being educated along with his sons. He was given access to Pharaoh's mystical teachings and learned from the secret teachings reserved for the King's heirs. He obtained the highest favor from Pharaoh himself dressed in Pharaoh's clothes. The Liberator was placed in the most favored position to learn the Universal Systems that were designed by the Higher Original Order. The story tells us that the

Promised Liberator was preserved by being placed in the river and floated in a basket along the river's edge. This Liberator who was called "Moses" was watched over by his sister to determine where the protected basket would end up. The story continues: Pharaoh's sister discovers the special child under the watchful eye of Moses' sister. When Pharaoh's sister discovered Moses and was determined to adopt him to be raised in Pharaoh's house, Moses' sister offered to assist her in finding a "wet nurse" who was Moses' natural mother to assist in raising the adopted child. In the Divine Order, Moses was actually nursed and nurtured by the (milk) knowledge that gave him the natural identity and knowledge of himself. The adopted mother thought she had accidentally found a perfect caretaker for the child, but the Universal Order was insuring that even in the alien house of Pharaoh, the child would grow based on the knowledge of his true identity. He had the protection of his intended assassin but unknowingly he grew from the breast of authentic Truth of who he was destined to be. Even though Pharaoh dressed him well as an adopted nephew, taught him well, treated him well, he grew to become the Prophesied Liberator from his oppressed people's greatest enemy. He was shielded in the enemy's house but he was fed from the milk of his own mother. The very complicated unfolding of this story shows that no matter how effective one may be in trying to disrupt the Divine Order, there is inevitable success in the Higher Order of things. The message in the "scriptural images" is to remind the oppressed and the oppressor that eventually Natural Moral Order will win and prevail.

In a related story, of the same theme, some centuries later, we find that another Liberator was born. As we indicated earlier, Herod was forewarned of the coming of this Liberator of the oppressed by his Wise Men. He made a similar decree that all of the young males should be killed and in fear that he might still miss this Messiah, he summoned his Wise Men again to go in search for the child that might have slipped by his plot of assassination. The Wise Men used Astrological science and determined that the prophecy had been fulfilled and when Herod was told this, he sent them in search of this special Liberator with the pretense that he wanted to come and pay homage to him as well. The Wise Men who were scientists and prophetic visionaries did find the child but because of their Wisdom that transcended the simple political ambitions of Herod, failed to return to tell Herod of their successful discovery. Since Herod's plan was still in force, Joseph, the biological father of the newly born Liberator Savior was directed by Divine Inspiration to flee Herod's land of oppression (the plantation) and take the child to Egypt. Here again in another version of the scriptural story, the Liberator was sent into EGYPT, just like Moses, to be hidden and raised in the special knowledge of the Egyptians. These two stories though centuries apart share some details that are too critical to ignore. We've seen how the oppressor attempted to destroy the Liberator by using the strategy of killing the young male children. In both instances Pharaoh and Herod's plans get fouled and the Liberator is concealed and raised in the Sacred High Wisdom of Egypt. Could it be accidental that both of these Liberators are raised under the influence of Ancient Egyptian (African) Science? If this is not accidental, then it must have an important meaning concealed in the Scriptural Stories to suggest that the transformative knowledge of human liberation must be found in Egypt. Even if we are not clear about what that knowledge happens to be, it is important to know that there is something special about this place that was named by its Ancient inhabitants, KMT (Kemet or the Black Land), and renamed by later explorers from Europe with the Greek name, "Egypt." We find that the Divine Order arranged for both Moses and the Liberator Savior called, "Jesus" both found refuge from death in Kemet and received their early earthly education there.

What does it mean to be a Man?

It's important to understand what it means to be a man who has been in a state of oppressive captivity in ignorance of their true identity. The image of becoming a "Man" takes on other dimensions beyond the usual processes of transformation that we have discussed in the earlier discussion of "maleness to manhood." As Black Men who have an extended history of slavery and oppression in America, we can see some examples of some things that impact on that developmental process of becoming Men. For one thing, once you declare yourself to be a Man coming out of captivity and oppression, you have automatically made a declaration of war on your former captors and oppressors. To be a Man is in complete contradiction to what was required to maintain you in a state of submission and captivity. Let's be very clear in this discussion that we do not assume that war is necessarily a violent attack, as we have seen in the "scriptural images" discussed above. Contrary to the modern fiction of the Western World, wars are not always fought with weapons. In fact, as we saw with the "Liberator Men" in the transcendent images described in this chapter of our discussion, the war that most terrified the captors

(Pharaoh and Herod) was the war of knowledge. It was in fact the weapons of knowledge that defeated the plans of assassination that were launched by the captors that led to the victory of the "Liberator Men" (Moses and Jesus.) When the Liberators brought the knowledge of manhood to the captive people, they stood in absolute and immediate defiance of their captors. The captors did not want the young "male" children to become Men which is why they decreed the children should be killed. The power of captivity demanded that the oppressed be seen as less than Men and incapable of becoming Men. In fact the Captor or Oppressor has defined his manhood on the basis of the inability of the captives to become Men. This was the danger of the Liberators who brought a contradictory message to the oppressed and freed them from their captors by teaching the captives how to be Men again.

There is no doubt that one of the most destructive forms of oppression is an outgrowth of racism. When a peoples' humanity is diminished and they are robbed of natural growth and transformation based upon their racial characteristics, even the scriptural stories aren't as horrible. In fact, when we look at the history of explorers (invaders) coming into Africa with radically different racial characteristics, Africans received them with warm hospitality because they responded to their humanity as a more important quality than their "strange" racial appearance. The same is true of the Native American people upon their encounter with the "racial pale face people." Even the stories of American colonization written by European American people acknowledges that Europeans would not have survived had it not been for the Native inhabitants responding to the humanity of the strangers rather than their racial characteristics. Both Africans and Native Americans were subsequently oppressed and violated because of this predisposition to judge people by their racial qualities and then to diminish their humanity. These victims of racism had never encountered other human beings who accepted the courtesy of visiting your home, receiving your hospitality, then claiming that you were an "inferior savage"; taking your house and claiming they "had discovered it." In an effort to identify the qualities of African Manhood, it is important to see that one of those characteristics is the fundamental respect for the humanity of other people and to transcend whatever physical characteristics they might have. The response to the fundamental humanity that you recognize in others is to treat them with respect, generosity and kindness. A frequent quote from a speech of Dr. Martin Luther King, Jr. is his declaration that Black people would be known by "the content of their character rather than the color of their skin." This declaration or vision is an expression of this fundamental principle reflecting Dr. King's African manhood. The response to different surface characteristics such as racial features is not to violently oppress them, take them captive and treat them as animals. The humanity in the Natural (African) Man resonates with the humanity in the stranger, even if he looks different on the surface.

Racism is a deadly and inhuman response because it intrudes on the natural human potential and expression of another person, simply because the other person looks somewhat different from the "racist." It is such an illogical system of thought that one must conclude that it is not simply intended as an attack on the victim of racism but it must serve some purpose other than to simply exercise the power of the racist. One possible explanation might be that the racist might be seeking the kind of immature power of "boys" who have not achieved manhood. Boys who are incomplete in their full development as Men would need to claim superiority by making others feel inferior. Men who have acquired their natural transformation would not have to gain their sense of supremacy or power by engaging in the kinds of practices of the racist who seeks to capture and oppress other human beings based on such childish distinctions like racial characteristics. Perhaps the racist feels inferior on the stage of human progress. Those who have achieved natural manhood can comfortably engage in the kind of humane hospitality and kindness that we have described as characterizing African Manhood. When we reflect on how much effort was put into distorting and excluding the contributions of the oppressed by oppressors from their captives and the exaggeration of the achievements of the captors, this explanation seems to fit into our model of Natural Manhood Development. We are aware that once the oppressed are taken captive, they are immediately blocked from access to knowledge which is the transformative power of growth. Whether it was slavery when to be caught with a book or learning to read was a major violation of the captor's rules of captivity or the kind of emancipation that we have discussed earlier that restricted what the former slave could learn, the control of knowledge was a key component of oppression. It is also clear that those "men" who struggled to restore freedom made knowledge or education a priority of their liberation battle.

This is also why we made the statement earlier in this discussion that when you decide to be an "African man", it is a declaration of war against those who value your captivity in the "cocoon of incomplete development." When your captors have based their power and superiority on your inferiority, they are invested in your remaining a boy or just a male. They have no objection to offering you assistance towards "emancipation" so long as you see them as the "Man", that is, the superior one. They will provide you a job, but you must be willing to accept them as the "Boss." They will award you advanced degrees in their Institutions of Higher Learning so long as you are loyal in your reference to them as the "Experts, Founders or Scholars." Any Expert or Scholar who challenges their basic assumptions about what is correct and adequate knowledge is viewed as illegitimate and will not earn their declaration of achievement. When you begin to suggest that John Henrik Clarke, John G. Jackson, Ivan Van Sertima, George G.M. James or other African Scholars had another interpretation of knowledge, then your sources and references are suspect because they don't validate the assumption of European superiority. You definitely do not want to suggest that Wade W. Nobles or Harriette McAdoo knows more about the African family than any of their sociologists or anthropologists who claimed the superiority of the European family structure. They will not accept the validity of the research of the brilliant multi-genius Senegalese scholar, Cheikh Anta Diop, who challenged their fundamental assumptions of the Development of African Civilization and culture as different and effective beyond the imagination of his European teachers of human development. With irrefutable multi-disciplinary evidence, he well documented the African Origin of Civilization but was required to do several re-writes of his dissertation at the Sorbonne in Paris because, his compelling evidence challenged the superiority of the European Explorers' knowledge. There was strong resistance to the recognition that this modern day "Intellectual Moses" had escaped the decree of assassination of African male children and had actually sat at the (European) Pharaoh's table, mastered his scholarship and found the message of African Liberation. Dr. Diop had come from a French colony in West Africa (Senegal) to the esteemed Institution of European knowledge, mastering History, Anthropology and Linguistic theories but still discovering the Liberating message for his captive African people.

A Declaration of War

To stand up as African men is a declaration of war! We must remember that this is not a game of sport and play that Boys manage to achieve. Standing up as Men is an invitation to enter a war against everything that you have learned to value in your undeveloped and captive state; it is a war with everything that your miseducation has taught you was most important. Mysterious things happen to Men who make this stand such as the sudden and premature death of Men such as Dr. Cheikh Anta Diop or the brilliant University of Chicago trained and defiant, Clinical Psychologist, Dr. Bobby Wright (in Chicago in 1986); the violent and still un-resolved questionable and premature assassination of Malcolm X or Martin Luther King, Jr. There is the risk of mysterious physical deaths such as occurred to these "Contemporary Moses Men" or the more subtle death to the academic scholars such as Dr. Carter G. Woodson who never received the kind of recognition or respect by the Academy or his own people because he challenged the educational distortions that he had received as a graduate of the Harvard University and formulated a concept that he called "miseducation", or training that failed to free the captive. You may never receive that most deserved Ph.D. that challenges the message of captivity. If you manage to slip by with the degree, you may never receive tenure or recognition even by those who you have used your scholarship to liberate. If you are in a corporation or some type of political organization, you may never get a promotion to a position of any real influence. In fact, you'll be lucky to be a part of the maintenance crew, regardless of how outstanding your work may be. This is because you have been recognized as being on the side of the opposition to the current holders of power. Defeats in settings that are/were established to keep you in captivity is victory in the war for liberation. Albert Einstein once observed very astutely: "We can't solve problems by using the same kind of thinking we used when we created them." In order for enslaved people to gain freedom, they must learn to think differently than they did as captives.

Manhood means self-definition

It's a declaration of your manhood when you begin to define yourself for yourself and by yourself. This is the first characteristic of a Man. No one tells you who your leader is when you are a Man. No one tells you what your ideals, or your goals should be when you are a Man. When you are a Man, you think for yourself and in your self-interest. No one has the authority to tell a real Man what his most pressing problems are. Based on your own research and observation, a real Man knows what environments are most conducive for his growth. A man determines that he has issues that are most problematic for him. Men understand that the problems that they face are an out-growth of particular circumstances that he faces and not someone else's description of his reality. When some "other man" tells you that your problem is because of a Black Woman or other Black Men, then you must be willing to see that the problems of captive men and captive women are problems that are a result of their condition, and they must define what that condition is. They cannot use the definitions imposed by other people's condition. Black men are not primarily affected by issues of Black youth versus Black adults; Black men versus Black women; class conflict; gender issues; Christians in conflict with Muslims or Catholics in conflict with Protestants nor Republicans vs. Democrats. The major conflict faced by Black Men in the Western world is a racial conflict rooted in the historical context of the captivity of African people and their systematic oppression based on race. It doesn't matter if the appearance of the problem may take on different manifestations to obscure the basic cause of the conflict, when the problem is defined by Men who know them-selves, they will conclude that the social, economic, psychological, spiritual and even many of the health problems confronted by Black people are a result of this historical relationship between the rac-es. Of course, very few of the victimizers will take responsibility for their role in this problem, which is why if any white people define the problems of Black people, they will attribute the cause of Black prob-lems and conflict to sources other than themselves. Even confused Black men who have internalized other people's definitions of who they are will attribute the cause to anything except this historical and on-going conflict of the races. Many people reading this analysis will conclude that their major problem is the opposite sex, some social, economic or physical condition or probably caused by another Black person. They will say with conviction: "Black folks give me more problems than White people do." This perception is based on what you might describe as a form of "plantation psychosis" whereby the oppressed have grown to see the privileged oppressor as their friend and the other oppressed people as their enemy. This is the success-ful distortion of reality that "Men" who know themselves can impose on those who have not come into their own manhood by develop-ing the power of self-definition. Those who have not become Men by defining themselves work towards their own destruction without realizing it. It's very important to understand that when you work in opposition to yourself and sustain the privilege of the oppressor, this is a form of "mental illness." Such people are not Men because they have voluntarily given up a fundamental privilege of manhood which is to define yourself. It doesn't matter how celebrated you are by your captor/oppressor; a man is "crazy" if he doesn't define who he is. This is why it is very important to have a "Black Psychology" that empowers you to define you, by you and for you. Some may say that this is simply a form of "reverse racism" but when you willingly accept other people's definition of who you are you violate your fundamental right to be human.

When you take back this right to define yourself, you take back your manhood and you become demonized by those who want you to remain a "boy", subject to their guidance. When courageous men such as Malcolm X or Minister Louis Farrakhan would make bold statements of self-definition about the condition or situation of Black people, they were looked upon as "dangerous militants."Neither of these men ever perpetrated any violence against anyone nor did they incite others to engage in any violence but they were viewed as "militants," only because they had no fear in defining themselves and the condition of their people. It doesn't take a great deal of courage to echo the ideas of other Men about the source of our problems, but to confront those other men with your self-definition to their face is considered to be "violent and militant." It's also easy to sit in a room with no one around but other Black people and suggest there is another way to understand the state of being Black in America, but when you do it publically you cause fear to those Black people who have not achieved their manhood and also to other Men who assume that it is their exclusive right to define the Black condition from an alien perspective. Such defiant self-definition, regardless of who is frightened by it, is the mark of a Man. This is not simply an issue of racial confrontation, but Men have actually gone to war and died for the right to define who they were. In other contexts, it's sometimes called "nationalism" and even the founders of the major world religions faced death in order to define themselves in relationship to the universe and Creator of the Universe.

People who have achieved genuine manhood are committed to defining themselves and if they feel that their power to do so is limited by other people trying to impose their definitions on them, will do whatever is necessary to preserve their right for self-definition. "Pharaoh's decree" to keep the children from growing into manhood is another example of preserving the ability of the powerful to define themselves as well as those that they want to control. As Men define themselves from their own perspective, they are able to access and maintain their power. Men build their Economic power based on concepts of Economics that enhance who they are. They build societies based on Sociological concepts that reinforce who they are. Concepts that strengthen Black families must come from effective Black Grandfathers who have raised outstanding families in the context of their circumstance. The best way to know how to raise Black children is to find out how Black mothers and fathers raised large families of ten or more children and every child grew up to be a good, strong human being with morals and constructive lifestyles who loved their parents and respected themselves. You can't get guidance on raising Black children by reading "Dr. Spock" or watching some reality television show of other people (or their imitators) giving you direction. You can't get proper direction by reading some "expert's book" on "Successful Child-rearing in Ten Easy Lessons" by somebody who never raised a Black Child. Black people must identify their own experts who have successfully achieved what you are trying to do. Some information, of course, can be generalized to any successful people. Black people need to study successful Black families and use their methods to determine what information is useful and fits the mold of what works. When we study Black families who raised a house full of children and all of them are successful, outstanding and aware people who know who they are and know where they need to go, then those are experts on Black child-rearing. It's important to have children who are aware of who they are, prepared to cope with the Europeans and their ways , but understand the African way and are capable of bringing both ways together for their success and the success of their people.

One of the major problems with African-American children is their preoccupation with imitating European-American children. A negative outcome of the achievements of desegregation and the "Civil Rights Struggle" is the creation of the first generation of African people in America who did not know that Black people are in a state of captivity. Every generation of Black people in America has known since the first slave ship landed that this is a dangerous place for African people. Each generation has understood that we have to change it, escape it or be prepared to expect the worst of circumstances because of their race. African people knew this well during slavery, during Reconstruction and even after Emancipation. Even when Africans had passively accepted their lives on the plantation, they kept praying for liberation. Even up until the end of the 20th century there was a continued aspiration to be free. Regardless how privileged an African-American person had become, there was a clear sense that something was wrong with the way that Black people were treated in the American society and there was a strong belief that something had to be done to change the society and make things better. It didn't require any argument from Black people that they were not free and that race was the basis of the problem. There was a strong conviction that desegregation, especially of the education system, would make a difference and this was accomplished, primarily, by subjecting African-American children to the Euro-American education system. Black people failed to realize that this was the fortress of White self-definition and along with the influential mass media; the evidence of African captivity began to be eliminated as generations of young people began to accept these new definitions of reality. Within a generation of this exposure, Black folks began to believe that White folks were better parents, teachers and human beings than they were. The power of self-definition was removed from the agenda of the Black community altogether and was replaced by European-American definitions of their problems and their reality. The textbooks and the television began to feed the minds of young Black children and "Pharaoh had successfully killed off" Black manhood and potential leadership for an alternative and self-generated message.

The concept of "Universal brotherhood" was not a concept from the recent history of European people. From the time that the Nubian King Menes of Ancient Kemet had unified upper and lower Egypt over 4000 years ago, this concept was the definition of humanity. As the invaders came into this Ancient Land they began to destroy the unification of humanity with their alien self definitions and began to fragment people into warring groups. The foreign invaders who were unaccustomed to such concepts of humanity introduced tribalism in the Ancient Land of Kemet, which was the civilized world at that time. Africa in its prime was a unified human brotherhood. This is why foreigners who came into Ancient Africa were warmly received as primarily human regardless of their different appearance. The warring invaders were unaccustomed to such unification within their definitional systems and under the influence of their power they brought division, oppression and captivity to the Land. The only hope of regaining the reunification of humanity is the restoration of traditional African definitions that saw people as fundamentally human rather than races or warring tribes in perpetual conflict based on superficial differences.

Men Control Their Environment

In addition to defining themselves, "Truly Developed Men" work to control the environments they live in. This kind of control is quite different from "domination", which implies the use of power over others. This control implies the goal of wanting to make sure that you and your people have access to the fundamental necessities of life. When they think of a food supply, they don't envision a Safeway, Kroger, Publix or even the corner Market that is controlled by someone else. Men envision an agricultural plan or a trade agreement with those who grow food, if you cannot grow it for yourself. Men should aspire to own or obtain some resource to give them negotiating power that will insure their access to basic foods for nourishment and survival. One man controls oil and he exchanges his oil resources for food. The idea is to establish a relationship so that someone is as dependent on you as you are on them and this is the trade relationship between "Men." When the only source of food that you have is the local supermarkets, then you are not a Man but a boy dependent on the resources of other men. What's even worse is a supposed-to-be "Man", depending on the government or someone to provide you the medium of exchange to obtain food, whether its food vouchers or charity, you are reduced to an even more dependent "boy" rather than a man for the necessities for survival. This does not mean that Men don't experience tragedies which require temporary dependence on others but it's a boy who has no aspiration to move from dependence to control of those necessities. When the only source of food and life necessities that you have any control over is to demand a hand-out from someone else or when you can't influence the provisions in the supermarket because the owner has a trade relationship with the resources that you control that he must depend on to stay in business then you are still a boy. You are like a child living in "Daddy's house". You may go into "Daddy's" refrigerator with "Daddy's "permission and get what Daddy will let you have, when Daddy will let you have it. If "Daddy" says: "Don't come in here anymore," then you can't go in that refrigerator anymore. You might think that couldn't happen so long as you have a food voucher card or even a limited amount of money in your pocket. If you can't influence the service of the supermarket because you are a man working with other men to control your environment, the owner of the Supermarket may only provide you with what he wants to provide in his store or may not let you in or he might close the store down completely if he chooses to. Your response to this possibility might be: "But, I am an executive at a prestigious company and this store may have been there for many years before you moved in the neighborhood, but do you have negotiating power or just buying power." Only Men have negotiating power that lets them buy selectively because of the trade relationships they have with the owners who depend upon their influence to maintain their power. Sharecroppers lived on their former master's land, but could only buy and make loans from the owner's store. The owner was the Man that had no trade relationship with the freed slaves so they could never own their land and were always indebted to the "Man" owner who they depended on for their survival. They could never own their land, shop at another store or become "Men" themselves because of the dependent relationship that kept them as boys for generations. It hasn't been that long since completely free Black people could only spend their money in the stores that segregated communities permitted them to buy in and could only purchase items the owners would sell them, because they were "free boys" and not "free Men" with trade negotiating influence. Even now in the early 21st century in major American cities multi-millionaire Black celebrities have reported instances where they were not permitted to enter exclusive stores that catered only to select White clientele. Many well-paid Blacks were frequently followed around major Department Stores by "Security Guards" because they are racially still treated as Boys rather than Men because of the absence of the trade negotiating power of Men who influenced their environments.

All of the major political powers that Black Americans took for granted during the post Civil War Reconstruction era in the late 1800's and after the Civil Rights Struggles of the late 20th Century could be taken away without cause. The right to vote and hold political positions after the Civil War was practiced on a wide scale by the former enslaved Africans in the recently defeated Southern United States. There were congressmen, state legislators and even Lieutenant governors throughout the South. Many Blacks were given ownership of large areas of property with deeds in their names. These achievements were maintained as long as the Union Troops were patrolling the Southern States and ensuring these rights. These were privileges insured by the power of White Men who had defeated and taken the power of the Southern White Men, whose defeat had reduced their ability to influence their environment. When there was a shift in White political power and the Troops were removed from the South, all of those privileges "given" to Black people were taken back and Southern Men reclaimed their "privilege" to define Black influence as they saw fit. They took away the powers of influence and citizenship that had been given to the former slaves and protected by the victorious "White Men" of the North. When the White political power shifted, the former slaves were left to re-discover that they were still

"Boys" despite what the White Men's Constitution claimed to have been their rights. African people could no longer vote, hold political office, own property and in most of the country were redefined as less than "Men." Black people were jailed, lynched, driven off of the land they had been given by the power of the Northern White Men. Men must gain and earn their power of influence and it cannot be given to you by other men or it can be just as easily taken away. In less than five years all of the gains of a twenty year period were eliminated overnight with the passage of "Jim Crow" laws (Woodward, 1974). Black folks who were previously "free" to go where they wanted to go, do what they wanted to do were suddenly not permitted to even walk on the same side of the street or drink from the same well as White Folks, who had re-defined their status. Unless Black Men systematically achieve and define themselves and their power as other Men do , the resources, access and power that Black people take for granted in this day and time can be just as easily taken away by the power of someone else to define you and their relationship to you. When European Americans changed their minds, Black influence was immediately eliminated. This simply means that no generation of Men can ever forget who they are and surrender their right to define themselves and maintain consistent influence over the environments where they live. No Men can doze into unawareness of letting someone else define who you are and what your priorities are. If Men give up their vigilance, they give up their manhood and run the risk of slipping into boyhood again.

Men Maintain Institutions that Define Their Reality

A priority of being a Man is to control your agenda based on your definition of what your needs are. Participating in the earned power of others does not mean that you have gained real power. Men do not set an agenda that makes their primary objective in life to get into another Man's house. Men must realize that the number ONE agenda item of their achieving manhood is to build their own house. It may be a small house at first; it may look like other Men's houses, but it must be your house if you are to be a Man. If you are going to be respected as a Man by other Men, you must have a house that you can claim belongs to you. Men's houses are built on the architectural blueprint of who they are, with a way of seeing the world that reflects the cocoon that gave you birth as a fully developed butterfly "Man" (with reference to our earlier metaphor) The schools where we educate our young must emerge from the same pattern of thought as do our "houses" or places that we live. Men should not put our primary energy into getting into other Men's schools. Men recognize that they need their own schools. This doesn't mean that any Man should be deprived the right of access to a public educational institution to master the general tools of a culture. Neither does it mean that any Man should be prohibited from attending any school that he chooses. Choice is the ultimate right of a Man.

As a people with a unique historical and cultural story, Men must recognize the need to have institutions that provide an intellectual normalization of who they are. Brigham Young University normalizes the Mormon experience. Mormons can go into any Institution anywhere and whenever anybody questions the legitimacy of the unique Mormon culture and thought, there are scholars at Brigham Young University who can attest within their Institutional framework the legitimacy of the Mormon perspective. Mormon students can refer to this Institution as a legitimate foundation for what they learn within the Mormon framework or any other Institution. Even though Jewish people have a prominent presence in most educational Institutions in Europe and America, the scholarship at Brandeis and Yeshiva Universities in the United States and at Hebrew Universities in Israel can be stalwart defenders of Jewish thought, Jewish political philosophy and the legitimacy of the "Jewish Homeland" in Israel. The scholarly Jewish "Men" in these Institutions provide the intellectual support and validation of the "Jewish House" among the Houses of other Men for Jewish students and in other Institutions. The only way that a people can operate effectively in a world of such cultural diversity is to have Institutions that define your reality and engage in the dialogue of human progress from your perspective. This also prevents other Men from taking your "House" of human rights as happened to the freed slaves when the thinking of certain groups of white "Men" changes. Until you have your "House" and your Institutions you can never be assured of permanent respect in other Men's Houses and Institutions. A course of study in a White Institution is not the same as having an African-based Institution that also offers other fields of study.

It is not "reverse racist" conduct to have publications and Journals that interpret the world from an African-centered perspective for African people. It's important to overcome the fear and irrational idea that only non-African (white) people can legitimize your perspective about you. This peculiar idea is another indication that a people are still "boys" and have not obtained authentic Manhood. Until one has Institutions that award doctoral and post-doctoral degrees approved by scholars in your Institutional framework, that states that the African perspective on human personality, economic development, social development and historical analysis is legitimate, you can never depend on scholars being legitimized in other Institutions and Houses can effectively validate your perspective. Other "Men" will make mockery of you for suggesting a perspective other than theirs. They will even legitimize and "train" African-American students in their Institutions to invalidate your perspective as illegitimate because it deviates from the European-American perspective. Without your own "House" and Institutions, you can only imitate the perspective that comes from an alien "House". With your own Institutions, other Men may disagree with your perspective but they cannot invalidate it and take away your rights to define and choose your self-definition.

Men Build Institutions to Preserve Their Resources

As we have described above, "Men" stand up and exercise control over their environment. Developing this power of influence requires that they must then have Institutions to preserve and continue that influence. Once the Man has established his "House" and "Institutions," they become major resources that must be defended and preserved. Defense in the most extreme sense becomes the military forces that preserve the Institutions and the Home, as we find in the nation systems. For the purposes of this discussion, such extreme measures are only illustrations of the need for self-defense to preserve the resources of Manhood. Justification for militant defense is beyond the scope of this discussion, but there are lessons to be learned from military systems that describe the significance of defending ones resources. Civilized "Men" should always seek to avoid offending other Men, but it is a mark of natural law that Men must exercise the right to defend themselves against malicious offenders who seek to destroy your humanity.

Men don't look for jobs but build Institutions that provide work and resources for survival! Boys look for employment in other Men's Institutions. Men don't try to pass on a legacy of a "job." They want to build Institutions so that generations yet unborn can claim their legacy. They want their descendants to look back at what they accomplished in securing a "House" that defines who they are with Institutions to continue the tradition of those achievements. Men strive to build ideas and concepts that stand and continue to generate expanded concepts for future generations to build on. Men seek to pass along "shoes" that future generations can walk along the path of human progress in, not borrowed ideas that were left by other Men. Every generation should want to pass on shoes that the next generation can put on and pass along with improvement. Every Man should want his children to stand in a reality of self-definition and resources of greater self-development that he helped to construct. Men want the next generation to build from a new plateau that you have spent your life trying to achieve. They should want to build Institutions that will stand, not for a few days or even a lifetime but for many lifetimes yet to come. Institutions must serve as the foundation for understanding realities that have not yet come into being. The highest hope of a Man is to build as the Ancient African Ancestors built: for Eternity. They constructed pyramids and systems of knowledge that current generations are still learning from. These Ancient Men were not satisfied with simply building a "House" but a blueprint for building that challenges future generations to reach for greater heights no matter what interference or attempted distortions may seek to destroy. This is the VISION that must guide the Institution building of each generation. Men should want to build with a sense of perfection and permanence firmly established in Truth of who you are and what humanity can be. Those Ancient African Ancestors set a model for Institutions such as this and this should be the inspiration that drives African Men. Men do not seek to simply be outstanding imitators of Other Men who built from the inspiration of who they thought themselves to be. That's the lofty Vision of all True Men. Men should want to build from the foundation of their Vision. One's Vision is not better or worse than another; your Vision is the unique perspective on the human experience as another Man's vision is his. From the air they are all beautiful butterflies that have been transformed through their cocoons to soar in the air and reflect the light of the sun.

The Return of Ra

African Men have found an expression through every conceivable religion of human kind. Certainly, the Traditional African Religions reflect a direct connection with the religious systems of Ancient Africa (Kemet or Egypt). In more recent times, African Men have found meaningful and authentic expression through the well-known Abrahamic religions of Judaism, Christianity (Catholic and Protestant) and

Islam. Though these latter religious systems were systems imposed by captors and oppressors of African people, "African Men" managed to transform each of these systems to reflect the self-affirmative definition that empowered them to transcend their captive states. The names of exemplary African Men who provided leadership out of captivity for their people are associated with all of these transformed religious systems. Judaism with Ben Amin and the African Hebrew Israelites; Christianity with Bishop Henry McNeil Turner and the Rev. Dr. Martin Luther King, Jr. and Islam with Noble Drew Ali, Elijah Muhammad, Malcolm X (Al Hajj Malik Shabazz) and Louis Farrakhan. In order for these religious systems to achieve the necessary job of liberation they had to be redefined by these Men who brought their transformed identities to the captors' forms of the religions. They were able to become effective Leaders of African Men by becoming transformed as Men and achieving the goal of self-definition that permitted transcendence from their captive state. If Christians choose to accept the captor's definition of the Christianity that depicts the "Son of God" as a Northern European with blond hair and blue eyes then that religion would simply serve to perpetuate their captivity. The Christians who recognized that the earliest practice of this religion were the people of Abyssinia or Black Ethiopians, were on the path to transforming the message in the religion for the liberation of African people. If Muslims view the authentic portrayal of the religion of Islam in the form of modern day Arabs who colonized and captured African people as slaves, then Islam would bring the same toxic contamination as a "white-washed" Christianity. The same is true if there are African people who accept the Jewish religion in the image of modern day Europeans who have claimed Judaism as their authentic religion. Each of these African Liberators portrayed their acceptance of the message of freedom in these religions in a presentation that reflected the captives' appearance and condition and not the appearance and condition of the captors. All of these religions bring messages of human transformation and liberation as do the stories of Pharaoh and Herod that we have repeatedly referenced in this discussion, but they must be transformed to match the condition and the appearance of the African people seeking liberation. What makes the system an "Orthodox" system is not some other people's definition of orthodoxy but your culture and the circumstances of your needs make them authentic, correct and orthodox.

As we conclude this discussion of "Transcending Images of Black Men," this is an appropriate place to return to describing the relevance of the stories of Herod and Pharaoh who were captors seeking to abort the rebirth of Manhood or the return of the Messiah.

If the objective is to offer a "Vision for Black Manhood," then Black Men must accept these stories as descriptive of them and not an historical narrative from some ancient or distant time. African Men must accept that these stories are pictures and Universal Truth that reflect the African experience here and now. African people are the Savior and the Messiah of this time who have been brought forth to restore humanity as a whole to its best. Just as the stories were originally presented to describe captive people who had the mission to restore and reform humanity, so is the African transformation from captivity and oppression. As the forces of opposition as portrayed by the Kings of the captors (named Herod and Pharaoh), did all that they could to prevent the transformation, the same is true in this time. The modern day Pharaohs and Herods have done all that they could to block the coming of the re-birth. Black men have been killed, mutilated, lynched, demonized and held in captivity of every conceivable form. Destructive drugs have been freely distributed, families have been systematically broken-up, education has been denied and distorted, constructive employment has been denied to African people and elaborate stories of the natural inferiority and necessary oppression of Black people is legendary in this contemporary version of attempts to block the coming of the "new birth." Now as in the times of these ancient stories, there was a failure to realize that when the time of the "New Message" has come, none of these devices will succeed in stopping it. The "Moses" transcendence and the "Jesus" birth will come despite what Pharaoh or Herod may do. The "Captor Kings" and their "Wisest Men" could not stop the "Divine Plan" that was set into operation and concluded before they even started to intervene. The "Author of the Plan" is a Transcendent Force in the Universe identified by the ancients as "Ma'at" or Universal Truth, Justice and Righteousness or by some as the "Divine Will." As the Ancient Pharaoh could not alter the course of the flow of the Nile River and its precious Messenger cargo, they could not create a plan that could outdo "The Divine Plan." At that time and in this time, one cannot alter the flow of the mighty Nile from its intended course. At the time of flooding, the Nile will flood and bring fertile soil to desert land. When the time for the re-emergence of Truth Consciousness has come, no mortal plan can stop it. It doesn't matter how hard alien forces may try to block the return of "Ra" or the sun of the new day across the horizon of the Eastern sky bringing the tidings of the new day, there is nothing that can keep it away. Ra will return!

We are already living in a time when the forces that have attempted to destroy the minds of new born African thought have sent out their decree. In spite of the evidence of mental slaughter and death, there are still outstanding new African Minds such as Cheikh Anta Diop, Asa Hilliard, Ivan Van Sertima, John Henrik Clarke, John G. Jackson, George James, Maulana Karenga, Wade W. Nobles, K.Kia Bunseki Fu-Kia, Anthony Browder, Ayi Kwei Armah and so many other "voices of Moses" leading the captives to the "promised land." These "Moses Voices" (some already have joined the Ancestors) spoke to the "burning bush" of Truth and those secrets that were so well hidden are once again re-awakening the consciousness that the colonizers and captors assumed were permanently silenced. These "Messengers" are awakening the consciousness of the captives and the oppressed with the keys to unlock the hidden records of their true identity and "Manhood" permitting them to know who they were intended to be. Despite the fact that modern day Pharaoh and Herod might have technology that was not even conceived in the earlier stories, when camels were the travel of choice and visual star-tracking was the means of mapping the intended victim, Truth has still eluded, drones, genomic and cyber tracking and has risen above the most sophisticated forms of deception and death. When the time for the "New Birth" has come, it will still come and return like "Ra" bringing the light of the new day.

3

EXODUS INTO MANHOOD

As we have discussed in earlier sections of this book, a "Male", a "Boy" and a "Man," are different manifestations but not the same thing. A Male is essentially a biological creature driven by instinct like any animal; a Boy is in the process of transition and a Man is a person that has arrived to a purpose and a destiny. When Men become really MEN and do not confuse their maleness or their boyishness with true manliness, they have come into a true discovery of what and who they were intended to be. There are real problems with those who confuse their biological identity with the mental and spiritual function they have as Men. There are problems for themselves and others for those who enjoy playing games, speeding wildly in fast cars while listening to loud music that distorts their actual hearing, who enjoy playing with girls rather than becoming partners with women and who enjoy the physical games and toys of life rather than being the steady and directed builders that are men.

Boys Masquerading as Men

The way out of the "masquerade" is through the process of "transformation" that we have touched upon in earlier sections. It is this process of transformation that permits oppressed and captive people to escape or transcend the destruction of their condition and rise to the horizon where liberation and freedom exists. It is at the time when the people are under siege by forces seeking to destroy their rebirth that Men are most needed in order to fulfill their destiny. When the captivity has moved from restraining the body to restraining the mind and there is no longer awareness that you have been blocked in your natural development, that Men are most needed. As long as a people are fully conscious that something is desperately wrong with their condition, there is a sense of rebellion in the people and efforts are made to change their condition, which requires the captors to restrain their bodies in order to keep them captive. When the oppressed and captive people begin to accept their situation and no longer want to be themselves but to become just like the captors and there is no longer a desire to become real "Men" that the time is ripe for a "Messenger" to come and remind them of their True identity. When boys begin to masquerade as men, their real identity has been lost and they think that boyhood is all that they are capable of becoming. One of the remarkable things about transformation is that it is a process of "nature" and Nature is the vehicle of the Creator. When the consciousness to fulfill our destiny (to be Men) has been lost, Nature produces a Messenger to restore the Message of Liberation and restore natural transformation. Even though this current deficiency in Men is present, and the captors have sent out a decree, his "Men of Wisdom" know that the Messenger is destined to come, despite his efforts to abort the process. The "Vision" that is given to us that inspires this discussion comes from faith in the processes of Nature that all vacuums in nature will be filled. Once the vacuum in "Manly Leadership" among oppressed people has occurred, the "Divine Architect" of the Universe causes it to be filled. The natural process of transformation restores the rebirth of Manly consciousness through the inspiration of a Man or Men who are given the Message of restoration. Whether it's through the transcendent process of a "Virgin Birth" of consciousness or direct communication with the Divine "I Am" through a burning bush on a mountain top, as the stories that we are following have suggested, the process of transformation restores the Man to tend the "garden of Eden" as in the story of Creation contained in the same Books or the image of the "Return of Ra."

There are many indications of boys masquerading as men and the need for a massive transformation in the African American consciousness. The problem of teenage pregnancy and the absence of responsible fathers in families is one such indication. The considerable number of women who experience feelings of hurt, unable to find companionship or reliable men, and having to shoulder full responsibility for the development of families, which should be a cooperative arrangement between Men and Women who have effectively been transformed. The fact that too many men (masquerading as boys) take relationships for a game to be played to perpetuate the lack of development among the people. Men strive to find ways to build for themselves and boys spend their time waiting for someone to give them a job or trying to avoid the serious business of working for themselves. Boys treat politics as positions in someone else's system of power and Men create ways of developing powerful influence. Boys confuse religion as debates over their belief systems and Men see religion as a way to foster relationships with Divine and spiritual Powers. Men construct institutions of learning and affirming who they are and boys masquerading as Men seek acceptance and legitimacy in other's Institutions of learning. Boys use their influence as Presidents of colleges and universities begging someone to keep the doors open, whereas Men who are Presidents maintain the mission of their universities, realizing that the doors will remain open so long as the Institutions offer proper guidance for future generations to know who they are. Scholarly Men, create definitions whereas boys seek tenure, status and acceptance by other's definitions of who they are. Boys use their scholarship to betray their people and Men define themselves by themselves for their people. Men think creative new thoughts and Boys memorize the thoughts of others. Boys masquerading as Men are spirits who have gone astray.

Adam and Abraham

The "true nature" of Men is not to be self-destructive. With the many, many, many negative stories told about African-American Men during this time of their captivity and oppression, there is a temptation to begin to accept that the deviance of black men ("masquerading as boys") is the norm of African behavior. It is very easy to begin to believe that the behaviors that we see in the media and hear on the news reports and even encounter in so-called "men" we meet is the True nature of African Manhood. "Boys masquerading as men" have many serious problems in their conduct and their behaviors and these problems are too often assumed to be characteristic of natural Black behavior. The horrific statistics of "Black-on-Black" homicide is considered natural for Black people. It's easy to believe that the epidemic of drug abuse and violence in Black communities is the nature of Black men. The high failure rate of Black boys in school (especially after the 4th grade) is assumed to be a characteristic of young Black men. For decades, there have been all kinds of conferences, studies, books and discussions suggesting that this kind of "deviance" of human conduct is actually the norm for African-American males.

It's important as we develop our "New Vision for Black Men" to realize that these demonic behaviors are actually "spirits that have gone astray." The authentic nature of African Men is just like the nature of all fully developed and transformed Men who have successfully passed through the stages of complete development. In fact, in the proper context, it is important to recognize that African Men actually set the precedent for humanity when we look at the growth of civilized human life. It was the "Men" from the part of the world that is called Africa who set the precedent for human excellence, human creativity and introduced humanity into its expression of effectiveness of the highest form. This deviance of self-destruction is a consequence of something of relatively recent onset.

No one can dare to call himself a real African Man unless he comes in the image of Adam. Who is Adam? Unfortunately, in our confusion some people are lost in their notion of recent fairy tale stories thinking of Adam as a semi-nude man of Caucasian characteristics wandering around in a mythical garden talking to reptiles hanging from trees. We have pictures in our minds of literal snakes, walking, talking and tempting the Northern European looking man in a tropical garden somewhere. They picture the "forbidden fruit" as an apple hanging from a tree and the subtle image is that the "Original Man" is this northern European, blond haired man and his mate of similar appearance. The distortion for the thinking of the African man that results in unnatural development and insane thought is that all evidence suggests that the earliest evidence of humanity was somewhere in the heart of the world that is known as Africa and if there is a literal image of this original man it would have to be a man of Black African appearance. These mistaken fairy tale images make it impossible for African Men to picture themselves as "Adam."

This discussion is not arguing that science should be made into God. Despite the value of science as a tool of observation, it is imperfect, otherwise, the discoveries of science would not continue to change over time and the scientists would not disagree with what they have observed. We believe that there is a "higher science" that offers clear and more complete explanations because it integrates all of the sciences (physical, mental and spiritual) and transforms them into a vision from a higher plane. There is considerable evidence to suggest that physical science offers a view or dimension of Truth (or "true being"), which is why physical science has transformed and expanded life. There is rather considerable agreement among various types of scientists that the earliest evidence of "Man" was physically located on the continent that we now call "Africa." This means that if we are going to select the best literal image of "Adam" he would have to look like someone who came from near the equator of Africa because it's there that the Anthropologists have found the oldest evidence of the remains of human beings. It would be very difficult to find a scientist who would argue the likelihood of the Garden of Eden to be in Norway or Scandinavia, where one is likely to find people with natural blond hair and the extremely pale skin color such as the images that are used to represent Adam and Eve. If there was a physical Adam in a physical Garden of Eden, the rich vegetation would most likely grow in Tropical Africa and its original inhabitants would have to look like African people who scientists clearly suggest are the only indigenous people who could have lived in this part of the world. Any literal image of Adam would have to look like a Black African man. If you fail to realize this then you are likely to become mystical, mysterious and lost in your aspiration for manhood. Adam and Eve (as one) is the prototype of "Adam." The story tells us that this "nature" of man was the "Keeper of the Garden."

There were other significant men who follow this image of "Man" in the religious scriptures who assume the appearance in the reader's mind of the same non-Black man Adam. There was another man who was responsible, we're told, for the original conception of religion as a "Monotheistic" system in whose image or form, this Man "Adam" was created. The implication from the distorted idea of Adam as physically a white Man, sneaks in the idea that there is only "One God" who looks like this man Adam. The idea is further expanded when we are introduced to the influence of another "Man" who as a descendant of Adam, who becomes the patriarch of the World's Monotheistic religions—Judaism, Christianity and Islam. Though there are other religions in the world, the idea is that they have residues of the more "primitive" polytheistic religious systems. In Judaism, this patriarch of the more "evolved and advanced religion" is called "Abraham." The opportunity to correct the distortions and suggest the African origin of this father of monotheism is lost again by ignoring the African Man, Akhenaton of the Nile Valley African nation called Egypt or "Kemet (KMT)". Actually images of this African man still exist in carved statues and pictures that show him to be a tall, slim, Black man who resembles the modern day Africans of Kenya called the "Watusi people". Even European historians share the historical records that indicate that Akhenaton was a King in Egypt (originally called: "KMT,") was severely criticized for reviving the earlier religious system of Monotheism. The name selected by this king is translated to mean, "the King of the One God." Not only did Akhenaton precede Abraham by many centuries but even at that early period, he was reviving an even earlier religious system. Under the Leadership of Akhenaton, there was a restoration of high arts and sciences in Kemet by the integration of these systems in his revival of the concept of the "Oneness of God" (ben-Jochanon,1970).

Even though Akhenaton's revival of monotheism occurred hundreds of years before Abraham's birth, the concept of the One God was considered to have been the "Way of the Ancients" in Akhenaton's time, there was no record of its beginning. The reader might ask: "What does all of this "historical mumbo jumbo" have to do with manhood in the 21st century. It is important to understand that Manhood is an achievement of power through identity. There are men of power in this world because they have a clear idea of who they are. They are powerful, economically, politically, intellectually and educationally. They are powerful in every dimension of human experience because they identify themselves with "Adam" and "Abraham." They exercise superior human power because they consider themselves to be the direct descendants of "Adam," "Abraham" and the original image of Man.

Who are the Fathers of Civilization?

If Africa was the location of the originators of the world's most pervasive and influential philosophies and religions, then "Men" from the continent of Africa must have played a significant role in the evolution of human consciousness on this planet called Earth. It would make logical sense to assume that if there are a people who must be identified as the "Fathers of Civilization," "Conceptualization," the "Fathers of Science" or the "Originators of Humanity;" as the "Patriarchs of the Human Race," then they must be from Africa. There is an important distinction between "his-story" and "our-story." When we begin to tell the story from our perspective, the story begins to take on another form. Not only does the story begin to take on another form, there is considerable evidence that the transformation begins to look much more like an African story, with considerable evidence without the need to stretch ones imagination.

The African Ancestors, who laid the foundation, left numerous markers, symbols, indicators, and maps. They seemed to have anticipated, that other people might come along and seek to take the birthmark of the early Founders. The monuments that they left seemed to declare: "Don't ever think that you can erase this: you may attempt to distort the story, but you cannot destroy an illustrated record that is both clear and massive." Europeans have done all that they could to erase the signs in Ancient Kemet and the Nile Valley Civilization that extends from the very heart of Africa, but the True story continually re-emerges. Despite efforts to disfigure the monuments, destroy the Colossus, erase the symbols on the Obelisks and the Temple; re-define the meaning of the Pyramids, they still persistent as images of Africans within the land of Africa. They have built dams to destroy many of the monuments; they have polluted the air and most of all polluted the perception and the minds of the world, so that Africans look at themselves and see someone else. They have gone so far as to fabricate myths that aliens came from out of space, landed in this part of the world and created these mighty monuments that record the story of humanity in Man's homeland of Africa. Such efforts are intended to keep the True Fathers from recognizing their identity. The Europeans would have the world believe that they are the Fathers of Healing, as the "Fathers of Medicine and of Science" in general in the person of the Greeks, Hippocrates and Aristotle. There is no greater art nor is there a higher science than that Science that heals the infirmed body. The influence of Hippocrates was so great in this particular science that over a thousand years later, the newly initiated healers of the body (or Medicine) are required to recite the "Hippocratic Oath" in order to enter into this renowned vocation. One of the reasons that all Men must tell "their story" is because the Europeans have established themselves as the starters, initiators and the ones whose genius gave birth to all significant events and all things must go back to them before you can be considered a legitimate "anything" or "anybody," you must receive their seal of approval. When they establish that "Hippocrates is the Father of Medicine," and you accept their story, then your son or daughter who aspires to be a Physician believes that he or she can only get through that door through the "Keeper of the Door" who fits the description of a European person. The "Keeper of the Door" is somebody who looks like the European, rather than the people of Africa who gave them their first instruction. The African person fails to learn that Hippocrates was a student of Imhotep, who preceded Hippocrates by several thousands of years. Imhotep, one of the earliest of African (Nubian) heritage who taught the Europeans their earliest lessons about healing based on African tradition. From all evidence that exists, the "Father" of human healing as we know it was this man of Africa who was actually celebrated as the source of Divine knowledge for many centuries after his death. This "Father" of healing was portrayed as a short, bald, black man with a large head. This same man pictured in numerous Temples and sacred Texts was "bald, of Black complexion, short stature and a very large head, " was also described as the Father of the earliest pyramid construction, master of military strategy and advisor to one of the earliest Nubian Kings; was also a writer of philosophy and poetry simultaneously (Hurry, 1978). The much later concept of the European notion of the "Renaissance Man" capable of multiple talents and skills in a wide variety of fields of thought was a replica of the "Imhotep Man", later considered to actually be a confidant of the Gods and was worshipped as such for many generations after.

In nearly every significant sphere of life, the prototypical "Man" is the African man. Many centuries later, "The Moors" (Black Men of Africa) restored the Europeans who had fallen into ignorance and paganism of the so-called "Dark Ages" with their fragmented concepts of the Unity of knowledge and the Unity of God. With their concepts of the unity of knowledge and science, the Moors brought Europe out of the "Dark Ages" and ushered in the Western Renaissance. (Lane-Poole, 1886). The Dogon people of Mali, in West Africa understood the structure of the planetary system thousands of years before there was the discovery of a telescope in Europe and the controversy of Copernicus who suggested that the Earth revolved around the sun which completely upset the European cosmology and the ideas of the Western Church. These same so-called "primitive" Black Men had a fully evolved understanding of the Sirian star system and its influence on the seasons of the Earth and the evolution of this galaxy long before Europeans knew there were other galaxies outside of the "Milky Way." The Dogon understood that there was a little star that ruled the big star. This was long before anyone in the Western World had even identified these stars and their patterns of movement (Griaule, 1986). But because Europeans understand their manhood, they are able to have Africans and other non-Europeans admiring their science when Black Men knew things thousands of years ago that the Caucasian Men have just recently discovered.

It is not accidental that most African people do not know this information about themselves. One of the ways that European Men maintain their claim of superiority over African and other peoples is not only by the focus on telling (even distorting) their contributions to world knowledge, but to conceal the contributions of other Men. The oppression, captivity, even enslavement of African People has been systematically enforced by claiming European "natural superiority" and African "natural inferiority". In order for slaves to be forced into involuntary servitude and to offer minimal resistance to their captivity is for the captors to know who they are and to conceal any information about the achievements of the captives (Akbar, 1996). In order for Men to become enslaved, they must be ignorant of who they are and the transformation of boys into manhood, must be blocked. The slaves cannot know their true identity. They have to wander around wondering and thinking they are somebody else, operating with a loss of consciousness. It is only under these circumstances that they can be ruled and controlled by Men who actually know who they are.

How then do the captives make an "exodus into manhood?" How do the enslaved move beyond the devastating attack on their manhood? Slavery effectively obscures the higher human aspirations and locks the enslaved into a state of unconsciousness. Beyond the physical captivity, slavery breaks the continuity with whom and what you were historically. The physical captivity begins the decline into a loss of your identity as Men, but the institution of slavery accelerates you into a death of consciousness and a loss of the "Man's Mind". There were two components to the loss of African manhood: The first step was the European Man had to demonstrate his superiority over the African mind, which was the revolt of the European "son" over the African Father. It was actually a revolt of those who had grown out of the knowledge obtained from their "African Fathers". It was a vengeful revolt of the barbarians who had come out of Europe to experience the flourishing civilization of the Masters of the Nile Valley. The envy of the achievements of the advanced African civilizations created a vengeful jealousy that motivated the revolt against the African Fathers that continues to plague them even unto this day. The motivation to prove their superiority over the Africans served as the genesis of the first step towards the captivity of African Men. Even though the institution of slavery began as a military attack and physical captivity, supported by economic, political, psychological and spiritual attacks—the underlying objective was to prove European superiority. The second step in this enslavement process was to create a sense of inferiority in the mind of the African and to convince him that his only ability to be a Man was to imitate his captor and reject himself as incapable of being a man.

The late and brilliant Senegalese scholar, Dr. Cheikh Anta Diop (1971,1981) explains that the "Southern cradle of civilization," which is the original Father of all human Civilization is the Africa Man. As the African man awakens to this reality, he can begin to understand what his destiny and responsibility must be. The awakening of this consciousness is the beginning of the "EXODUS."

The "Real Exodus"

First of all, it is important to understand what the Exodus really is before it can be made by African Men. Most people believe without question that the "Exodus" is a story of European Jews leaving their Caucasian captors and coming out of so-called "Egypt" (without mentioning that Egypt is located in Africa). The historical record is very clear that there is no evidence of European people ever being held captive by the native inhabitants of the part of the world that we identify as Egypt. The Egyptians were very detailed in documenting all aspects of their history, both in victory and in defeat. There is no evidence in any Egyptian writings of a massive captivity and subsequent migration of European Jews the way that it is fictionalized in the cinema and communicated in Judeo-Christian scriptural stories (ben-Jochanon, 1970). This idea is highly popularized in all of the Abrahamic religious scriptures, and in Western Literature. This story must have some significance since it has been told over and over among numerous religious groups. So, with its great popularity, it's important that we know what this story means. Who was leaving Egypt and where were they going? How did they get there and how did they get out? These are all legitimate questions since so much of Western history is based on the answers to these stories. What does this story mean? How did this multitude of people get out of captivity? Where did they go and who guided them out of their captive state? What were they escaping from when they left and where were they "promised" to go? It's important to know the real story of the Exodus.

Let me boldly suggest that the story of the Exodus is a Universal story or metaphor for the allegorical process of initiation or transformation from the captive state of Boyhood to the "Promised Land" of human freedom known as "Manhood." The Exodus is a collective picture story of the process by which the incompletely formed human being moves from a state of captivity or incomplete development into the full capability and freedom of their intended human maturation or completion. In finding ones full human capacity the limited captive being discovers the "Promised Land" of His full Humanity. The powerful story of the people escaping from the captivity of their uncompleted development across the desert transforms and completes them in their humanity. They escape from the limitations of the cocoon of their potential "Being" as boys to become the butterflies of true Manhood. The "Exodus" is a reminder that every generation and every person must be transformed and initiated by escaping through the desert of unawareness, self-limitation to find the freedom of self-consciousness that will let them fly and achieve the full benefits of their destiny.

If this is the "Real Exodus," then what is required of those who are going to make the journey or escape from their limiting human captivity? Let's return to the story of the scriptural Exodus: First, we are told that the captives, in order to get free, had to be "called" by their true name and reminded or taught who they really were. (That is; they had to be identified.) Who are you as a person and as a people? What is your true identity? Are you one of those who sees himself as simply like the "Egyptian captor?" Are you one who shares the partial freedom of the "Egyptian Captor"? Are you a part of the structure of Pharaoh's kingdom and power? Do you have equal access to the wealth of Pharaoh? Are you committed to the pedagogy and the educational process of the land (mind) of Egypt? Are you an equal in the government and authority of Egypt? Do your opinions and your story have equal influence in Egypt? Does the Egyptian narrative of who they are (their history) include the totality of your experience? These must be the initial questions that those who are captives must ask in order to distinguish themselves from their captives.

The Chosen People

The task of those that must be achieved by those who choose to join the "Real Exodus" into manhood is to know clearly and distinctly who they are. Who is the African Man? We must look at those men who have come as leaders like Moses who called the captives out of their Egyptian captivity. They will not be people of great popularity to the Egyptian Pharaoh as Moses was viewed as a traitor to the captor's vision. They will be people like the Honorable Marcus Mosiah Garvey, the Honorable Elijah Muhammad and the Honorable

Noble Drew Ali whose direction radically transformed the identity of African captives as Moses radically transformed the identity of the people that he led. In the context of self-definition and self-identification, these Men of the 20th century must be viewed as African "Saints," or "Prophets." Why do I make such a bold statement? These "African Saints" took the lives of tens of thousands of captive people and transformed them with their Messages of redefinition. Though they were all despised by the Egyptian Authorities and declared enemies to the reigning Pharaoh and to the "Egyptian Divinities," they took "males" and "boys" out of prisons and jails and removed dope from their bodies and self-destruction from their lives and transformed them into upright men of dignity and self-determination. They were considerably more effective in transforming lives than were the Egyptian-trained psychologists, criminologists, ministers and social workers. Even now these "Egyptian degreed" and Pharaoh-appointed counselors and experts do not have a technique to transform junkies, recidivist criminals and self-destructive boys into men. I challenge "Dr. Social Worker and Dr. Psychologist" to take a prostitute and make her give up turning "tricks" and start turning on the light of civilization. Which of Pharaoh's experts could have taken a "Negro boy Boxer" from Louisville named "Cassius" and transform him into "Muhammad Ali" who fought for civilization and human dignity all over the world?

In order to make the "Real Exodus" it is important to know the true identity of a Man. The Honorable Elijah Muhammad (1965) brought a "Message to the Black Man in America." The Honorable Marcus Garvey (1967) said emphatically that a "Man is the individual who is able to shape his own character, master his own will, direct his own life, and shape his own ends." There is nothing ordinary about a real man. The Man who was made to be the "Keeper of the Garden" (Adam) shaped in the image of his Divine Creator was not ordinary. He was not there on the basis of "instinct" or habit, but on the basis of "Will" and Higher Inspiration. A Real Man's behavior doesn't change when the seasons change or the phases of the moon change. The Real Man is dictated to by his character, his intelligence, his moral sense. The Real Man is not dictated to by his limited nature but by his higher nature. Sex, wealth, games, toys, physical power, appetites and physique don't dictate his identity. His "Will" stands over all of these drives that push and pull at his lower nature. Nicotine can't control him; caffeine does not drive him; fleeting passion and material influence cannot contain him; dope in any form cannot master him; the latest form of technology toy or automobile is not his master. The Man understands that his true identity is in his will power, in his character, is in his drive for self-mastery and self-creation. This means that the Man who knows his true identity is free already. Your manhood is not what goes on the body, but is the power within the body. The True Man maintains his manhood with shoes on or off; in workman's clothes or royal robes; walking, riding or flying; in solitude or hailed by multitudes because his human dignity, his character and his will is his Manly identity.

We can further define the Nature of Man by making reference to another Scriptural Story. When the Divine Creator (according to the Genesis) breathed into the nostrils of man, the breath of life, He became a "living soul" and was endowed with the authority of the Master of Creation. The scriptural stories suggest that Man was made in the image of the "Lord of Creation." This is another metaphor we are only accustomed to hearing parts of in our religious teachings and we seldom hear this kind of language in educational settings. This description of the "Nature of Man" is not only a Sunday school picture story; it is psychology, anthropology, science, mathematics, music and the arts. This description is also a statement about political freedom and even the language of revolution. This understanding of the Man's True Nature is the map to human freedom. The human being should never descend to the level of accepting the identity of a slave to another man, woman, substance or object, but He should always be in full possession of his senses with the truest knowledge of himself. Societies have seriously distorted this Divine Nature of Man by dividing them into social, psychological, intellectual, linguistic, races even genders and classes of distinction. We were not made in these hierarchies of distinctions. We were created as Man in the Highest Form and sense, even though we are so misguided that we can hardly identify a real man in our contemporary world, whether it's in a place of religious faith or political power.

In the course of time, we find that only a certain type of man has been able to make good as true "Lords of Creation." We find such Men building nations, governments, empires, great monuments, commerce, industry and institutions of learning. Only a limited selection of men have realized the power given to them and have exerted every bit of it to their own good and to their posterity. While on the other hand, as Garvey (1967) said: " Four hundred million Negroes who claim a common fatherhood of God and brotherhood of man, have fallen back so completely as to make us today the serfs and slaves of those who fully know themselves and have taken control of that which was given to all in common by the Creator. Garvey (1967) goes on to say: "I desire to impress upon the 400 million men of my race, that our failings in the past, present and in the future will be through our failures to know ourselves and to realize the true function of man on this mundane sphere." Garvey's basic principle was not to take the Black man "back to Africa," but it was to take the Black man "into the desert," to re-locate himself. Garvey's basic principle was a call for the "Exodus." He knew the scriptural story, too. He knew the power of mythology and if you introduced a universal mythological symbol, you could begin to activate a powerful archetypal image in the collective minds of an oppressed and enslaved people and mobilize them to re-claim their humanity and identify with the symbolic enslaved "Jews held in captivity in Egypt." In order to make this happen it was critical for them to know who they were. Once that image was internalized and they began to believe in themselves, they would be able to make the Exodus. The Black men of the world or the "Universal Negro Improvement Association" had to believe they were somebody who was special and "Chosen." Chosen by whom? They were chosen by the "God of the Universe." They would have to give up the aspiration to be chosen by Pharaoh and realize that they were chosen by the God of the Universe. They would have to be chosen; not by Moses or anyone of the small world they had come to accept as "real." In order for the Black Man to become free, they would have to believe that the Laws they were following were the Universal Laws of their true nature. They would have to understand that these Laws were the Laws of the Ruler of the Universe and that they were a part of that process of Universal Truth. The words, "Chosen People" were not Words that made them superior to other humans but they were the words that defined their humanity and they were of Truth and a manifestation of Truth. "God-Chosen" people means, "God-Choosing people." The qualification that makes a people chosen is not their racial or ethnic make-up. The God of the Universe does not select certain people because they have more or less Blackness in their skins. With a Will and Intelligence, you are given the option to choose Truth. Every human being is chosen when He is given life. If you breathe in this atmosphere, you are chosen; if you eat the food that grows from this earth, you are chosen. The quality that distinguishes one people from another is their choice to select the Righteous Path for life. When you choose your correct identity as one who chooses Truth, this makes you distinct from those who choose an alien or a self-destructive life course. Selecting life and the Life of Growth and Transformation is the beginning of the process to move you from captivity in Egypt to go into the "Promised Land" through the course of the Desert.

Fear of Going into the Desert

People are usually quite terrified of going into the "desert" because Egypt offers such security and wealth. In Egypt, you can have secure employment working on a job that protects someone else's reality. You have good "benefits" and the security of a familiar job. In "Egypt" there is full employment even when there is unemployment, because of the security of the welfare system. Even the homeless have access to the infrastructure and the public works of Egypt, which prohibits them from engaging in self-sufficiency as will be the case in the desert. So, even the enslaved person finds security in his captivity and he is frightened at any thought of the desolation of the desert and the need to depend on himself rather than the master or the captor. When you move into the desert, the conversation shifts from participation to independent creation and this is a very frightening conversation. When the Honorable Elijah Muhammad (1965) challenged the Black man "to do something for himself," he was inviting the former slave to enter the desert with nothing less than the vehement opposition from the majority of Black People. Mr. Muhammad and Mr. Garvey were raising the frightening challenge of Moses calling the slaves into the desert. When you change the conversation from: "let us into your schools;" to "let us build our own schools," the opposition came. When these "Moses Men" encouraged the Black man to start his own government rather than demand participation in Egypt's government, there was strong opposition because this would entail an Exodus into the Desert. It's frightening for the former slave to anticipate giving up the luxuries that his captivity has given him access to, such as the Mercedes, or the Cadillac that the master has permitted the slave to purchase for exorbitant and extravagant costs. In the desert, the distinction of being an illegitimate distant relative of the Pharaoh will serve no purpose and no one will find it prestigious that you may have DNA to connect you with your former captors, the Egyptians. The prospect of having to plow the land, to grow your food or shear the lamb to get wool to stay warm is understandably terrifying to the captives that have grown comfortable with credit cards and the former masters' grocery stores and various "Marts or Malls" and fast food on every corner, far removed from the actual farm from which they came.

When one goes into the desert, he must begin to answer some very serious questions. Questions such as how to teach the young people to imitate our wisest elders in order to transmit our best human characteristics must be answered. How do we preserve the historical identity and dignity that human beings have acquired over time? How do we begin to transmit to our young people a sense of responsibility and commitment to the human community and how do we encourage them to "come home" to us rather than taking their abilities and brilliant minds to somebody else? How can we insure that our daughters will become the kind of mothers that will cultivate their children to be dignified, respectful, grateful men of their own culture? These questions can be answered only if we know who we are. We must preserve the memory that our ancestors were men who survived and endured slavery, but who also set the prototype for the origin of civilization and teach this as a lesson that builds confidence while maintaining humility and not ethnocentric arrogance.

Men, reconstructing their lives through passage in the desert must learn to be themselves again. In slavery the captives lost the meaning of real power and developed a slave's distortion of power. Real power equips a people to be self-determining because doing for oneself rather than seeking favors from the master is authentic independence. When a people are truly free, they have real independence to develop economic enterprises, for an example. Economic enterprise does not mean getting a good job from someone who understands his freedom, or developing a "Stop-and-Shop Bar BQ stand." Free people need more than hair salons, barber shops, funeral homes and sandwich shops. There is nothing wrong with starting at this level of satisfying personal needs, but an Enterprise is what Madame C.J. Walker established as a national chain of hair salons and taught people how to offer this service, and develop similar chains. This is why she became the first Black woman millionaire after starting off in the "desert" of her small kitchen. As we have said above, the "Exodus" means to move into the desert, but it must be done with faith and belief in who you are. It takes faith in the forces that brought you into existence and a belief that your presence in the world is by no means an accident. It requires you to know and understand the lessons that have been learned and the lessons taught by the collective experiences of your people. Entering the desert, you must internalize the words of the familiar church hymn that say: "Through many dangers, toils and snares, I have already come . . . ." The freed slaves must know where they have been already and how those experiences have prepared them for these struggles. African Americans were born in different stations of life:

some with a so-called "silver spoon" in their mouths meaning that they were born into conditions of comfort and well-being; others were born with a "bronze spoon," or "no spoon" in conditions of abject poverty. Some people have known hardship and personal struggle and others have no familiarity with any kind of hardship. Regardless of one's individual social economic conditions, as a people, we have become something of value despite having been reduced to nothingness in the collective condition of African enslavement in the Western world. The collective condition of all Africans in their captivity is that they were reduced to being less than human. In the course of 400 years, African humanity had been violated in the most fundamental sense of self-respect and self-determination.

It's very easy to forget these dehumanizing conditions when you look at African Americans now. From the position of leadership of the American government, in the Arts, and the most prestigious European American Institutions, the enslaved African descendants are highly dignified, prestigious and some African-Americans speak, write and teach the English language or other languages of their historical enslavers with greater proficiency than some of their captors' descendants. These descendants of captivity can be found in every arena of the Culture of their former enslavers from the peaks of computer science, to pilots of aircraft into outer space. The descendants of slaves are esteemed professors in the loftiest European American Institutions whether it's the Ivy League in America or at Oxford in England, the University of Berlin in Germany or the Sorbonne in France. The children of these former slaves march out of these Institutions with honors of magna cum laude, summa cum laude and in every imaginable dimension of laudatory celebration of their mastery of their former captors' educational Institutions. There is a lesson in these examples of achievement: Certainly not even most Africans can claim this level of accomplishment, but the lesson that must be acknowledged is that if one of the former slaves can reach these lofty heights, it means that there is a force that is able to transcend the reality of African captivity. No matter what force may still be attempting to destroy and diminish African humanity, that Superior Force is capable of overcoming it. One Black Ph.D. in physics from the prestigious M. I. T. (Massachusetts Institute of Technology) has already defied the theories and speculations of Western socio-psychological theories that would suggest innate African inferiority. Just one self-respecting, self-determining African at the head of a European-American government demonstrates that Black boys and Black girls are in fact "fully capable." There may be failures, but the failures take place in a system that does not recognize African competence and genius. The failure exists in a system that fails to let those young people know their own competence because of an insufficient number of role models that can demonstrate their capability. These African achievers are able to identify with an alien knowledge, an alien mind, and an alien intellect and still excel beyond the aliens themselves, within their own system. This is truly remarkable! African people don't realize how great they are!

The "Secret Door" in the Pyramid

In order for the "Chosen People" to receive their divine rewards, they don't simply need faith but they must also have knowledge. Knowledge of their history as oppressed people, demonstrates that their salvation is certain because of what they have already endured. The oppressed African people in contemporary time realize they have already endured so much worse than the residues of oppression that they experience in this time. The oppressors have got to come up with something more destructive than the bigotry, prejudice, discrimination and superficial oppression of this time. When the oppressed people have knowledge of their history they realize that they have already had their names, their culture, their minds taken away from them—but they cannot have their spirit taken away because it belongs to something much bigger. The oppressors could not take the spirit of the captives because they were not capable of comprehending the force that had sustained them under the conditions that were intended to mentally destroy them. The captors did not know how to get into the "secret passages of the human pyramid." The oppressors were permitted to only see the outer structure of the "pyramid". Only the builders knew that the Great Architect of the pyramids had structured passages that gave access to the Higher Reality of the invisible dimensions of the pyramid. When they invaded these sacred structures, they didn't know that there was a secret door that went to the invisible passages of the hidden pyramid. It is there that the oppressed people were able to keep their spirits alive. It is there through all of the outer devastation of the African identity, they were able to maintain their life. Now, as preparation for the exodus begins and those who are prepared (made aware of themselves) can begin to choose the Higher Authority of their True identity, they can emerge from the hidden passages of the Pyramids. The "Prophets" have declared to the Pharaoh to "Let my people go!" They must go to an Independent thought pattern and a new identity. They must restore Africa to the center of the spiritual world where it once stood before the coming of the oppressors. They must arise from the hidden passages where their true human nature has been hidden in exile.

It is not necessary to advocate a form of vindictive reverse racism in order to be restored to the natural humanity of the captives. Such a "reverse racism" would argue that "I am good in my Blackness because you are bad in your Whiteness."The essence of the human being cannot be distinguished according to physical racial characteristics. Racial characteristics are no more than environmental manifestations of physical expressions. Race is the outer veneer of illusion that covers the pyramid in its physical form. Unfortunately, for too long the world has been structured in this superficial and unnatural way. Of course, if you are captured in a world that is structured based on this faulty model, then it must be addressed while you are in captivity, but one can easily get mentally captured in this distorted world reality and try to take it with you when you begin the Exodus. While in captivity, you might try to impose another reality and adopt a point of view that argues: "I'm color-blind, humanity is all alike; we are one humanity." Such a perception will leave you vulnerable in a world distorted by racial designation. Try to tell a "Klansman" your liberated perception and you will meet with an untimely demise. Try to convince an employer who has been indoctrinated with the racist distortions, who is about to decide on your promotion when his fellow race member is competing against you in your so-called "racial objectivity" (and often greater competence) and you will quickly discover that race is real in Pharaoh's kingdom. In fact, "Mr. Misguided Former Slave:" get on your soap box and argue about the "oneness of humanity" and the irrelevance of race consideration and you will find yourself crying in the soup line begging for a hand-out. Many misguided former slaves really believe that their former "masters" sincerely love them. They will make statements such as: "I am not interested in all of this racial stuff; we are living in a 'post racial society; that 'Black stuff' was relevant in the 1960's and 1970's ; we have now transcended that with all kinds of Black political leaders even in the deep south." Actually, African people had transcended "race" even before the 1960's but we had to reincarnate in the modern world in order to restore the concept of humanity for European American (white people.)

Do you think that Martin Luther King, Jr., and all of the Civil Rights Leaders in America were teaching Black People? He didn't have to teach African Americans the value of freedom? They had known freedom long before their captivity in the Western World. It wasn't necessary to teach fairness to people who had been treated so unfairly. He didn't have to teach the value of justice to a people who had been treated so unjustly. It wasn't necessary to teach the dignity of human beings to a people who had been treated with such indignity. He was trying to teach those who had violated the codes of civilized life to a people who had so viciously violated those fundamental codes of civilized human conduct in their treatment of the captive Africans. The victims of human oppression did not need lessons in respect for other human beings but for those whose history had been filled with examples of oppressing other humans due to their race, nationality, ethnicity, religious faith, gender or other social/physical characteristics. Unfortunately, as a result of sharing the same cultural environment under the conditions of their captivity, some African people became contaminated by their flaws and began to believe that superficial physical/social characteristics were more significant than the human inner qualities that Africans had collectively elevated to a science. Sadly, the African captives began to see themselves in the negative light of their captors and internalized not only this inferior perception of the human being, but identified with its invalid conclusions even about themselves. They learned to accept the inferiority of Black people and believed that a Black politician was incapable of conducting government on their own. The confused captives believed that a Black Attorney could not properly defend you in the court systems, or a Black doctor (if he attained such achievement) could not heal you if you were sick, despite his credentials. Some African captives actually believed that ice sold by white captors was magically colder than the ice sold by a Black vendor. As I have discussed in other settings (Akbar, 1996), Black people became so confused by this system of White supremacy domination that they lost faith in themselves and all African people. African people internalized the system of white supremacy domination that the African struggle and culture was intended to teach their captors.

This is why the captives have to make the exodus into the desert. Not only do they need to escape the influence of their captors but they must also escape the influence of their captivity. In the desert the captives have to re-discover their faith in themselves and to understand what made them who they were prior to their captivity. There is actually not one enslaved African who was supposed to have survived this captivity. Yes, there are Black junkies, murderers and every imaginable form of self-destructive abusers. When you fully understand the kind of self-hatred that creates these self-destructive behaviors, all of the former captives should be free of these disorders. It's easy to identify every imaginable form of crazy Black person. There are wife abusers, rapists, even child molesters and some of everything among the Black people, but look how African humanity was violated during the years in captivity. In spite of this, look at the genius that has survived even in captivity. Despite the captivity there are brilliant scholars, lawyers, doctors, plumbers, preachers, theologians, artists of all forms. There are mothers and fathers who love their children and build exemplary families despite the destructive influences of captivity. They are able to transform the minds of young children from the most adverse conditions and attacks against their humanity. There are examples of men who have broken their backs in order to send nine or ten children to the best schools the Western Society can produce with a commitment of advancement for their own people. These are not just isolated examples but in some of the most destructive environments, it's the rule for Black people.

It is important not to be confused with the negative and predictable examples of human self-destruction among Black people. The captives have learned some deadly habits from their captors. African people were not molesting their children prior to enslavement. Suicide was unheard of in most African societies and even under the destructive conditions of slavery the ultimate form of self-destruction in the form of suicide, became more common among the captors than among the captives. African people began to practice such alien and destructive habits after they were exposed to them under the inhuman conditions of slavery. When one considers that Africans have been "free" in European-American society for just over a hundred years which is less time than they were captives, it shouldn't be surprising that many of the destructive habits of this alien culture have affected them in a rather negative way. The power of African resilience and resistance is demonstrated by the achievements of the formerly enslaved people and not by the failures or handicaps of living under such inhuman conditions. This ability to achieve regardless of circumstances is in the African people because it is the power that made it possible for them to survive. This is the power that Africans must rediscover as they make the Exodus. The capacity to transform devastating and inhuman circumstances into triumphs of excellence is the hidden information that will be revealed when they go into the desert.

From Self-Knowledge to Self-Mastery

Once the captives have moved into the desert, they begin to take on an independent identity, which must first occur through the re-cultivation of self-knowledge, which extends from the development of self-mastery. The African Man must re-discover that he is "Adam." Adam means that your essential character is in your ability to be a "leader" or "ruler". Not only is this leadership over the earth as the Biblical picture of Adam, but initially over the "earth" that is yourself. A leader or a ruler must first be a follower of certain Divine or Natural principles as the Biblical or allegorical Adam had to follow the instructions of His Creator. The restored Adam is required to know that nicotine, alcohol or any vice of the lower self is ultimately weaker than the power that is in your character (who was "made in the image of God.") In the desert, Adam must rediscover that any of the qualities and appetites that he acquired in the "Egypt" of his captivity is weaker than he is. If he doesn't realize his superior strength of character, then he doesn't realize his true capability as a "Man like God." Once you know who you really are and realize that you are not a servant of Egypt, and then you know that you can do whatever you CHOOSE to do. African men have demonstrated this over centuries of achievement. The Original Creator took nothing out of the void (a black hole in the cosmos) and constructed all that is. The African Adam took out of the barren land and constructed all that was original civilization. African men built agricultural estates. They carved monuments out of the sides of mountains that stood undisturbed for over three thousand years; they recorded the processes of nature and life, and left written documents for those coming behind them. Most importantly Africans removed the consciousness of men out of triple darkness of ignorance and transformed it into the light of human intelligence, dignity and morality and taught humanity to stand up as a rational creature guided by the Sun of God, Himself. These are examples of what African men along the Nile River did before most of the world had a spoken language.

When you go into the desert you must reestablish authority over yourself. Self-mastery becomes the step after gaining self-knowledge or self discovery. This is important because it is only when you restore the ability to rule yourself (kingdom) that you have the ability to rule "The Kingdom." The father who is weak in the home has no authority in that home. The father who is unable to be respected in his home has no authority. His wife doesn't listen to him, the children don't listen to him, and even the dog won't listen to him. There is no way to fool the people who live in the home. If they see you as incapable of controlling yourself by consistent habits of weakness, they conclude that you are weak. It doesn't matter what you may say, they see you and react to your hypocrisy, even if you go to church and out-sing everybody in the choir; in the home you are seen in your weakness and your inability to control yourself. Whether it's your inability to control your drinking, smoking or any of your habits of self-discipline, they see you in your true form in the home. They may listen to you boasting to your friends about your manly authority but see your inability to pick-up your dirty socks when you take them off. Those who see you in your house realize that you are simply a lying hypocrite when you boast about your authority and your strength. Your actions speak much louder than your boasting song.

Boys cannot pretend to be Men in their homes because their actions contradict them. Boys are always playing games and don't realize that their actions give them away as not being the men they claim to be. Too many fathers in an effort to model "manhood," end-up modeling "boyhood" instead by their actions. Even with the significant number of Black fathers who are absent from the home, the few who are there, too often are poor examples because they have not learned to be Men. They will take their sons and show them what the "boys do." This is often a secret rendezvous with another woman that they take their sons along as an excuse to get away from the son's mother and inviting the young boy to be his secret conspirator in infidelity as a demonstration of what "men" do. Sometimes, they will take them to adult settings and introduce them to alcohol consumption in the "club" or "bar" while giving another example of what men do when they are away from the home. They are actually teaching the boys how to remain boys, which is their only concept of what it means to be a man because the fathers have not evolved to become true men themselves.

Under the most desirable conditions of growth, Men should want to model the best examples of responsible manhood. They want their sons to be in charge of the real world and not in charge of boyish games. These effectively evolved men understand what it means to be in charge of the world they live in and they want them to see examples of Men who are in charge of the world. These fathers, who have acquired authentic manhood, understand that their sons will grow into the kind of men they see around them. Even though these fathers may have boyish habits of their own, they don't want their sons to see them at their worst but at their best. They carefully separate whatever boyhood entertainment they might enjoy from the environments that they expose their sons to. Even though these evolved fathers are far from perfect, they realize that their sons will aspire for perfection if you expose them to perfect or out-standing models of manhood. This doesn't mean that in order to be a man, one must become a "Monk" who never finds enjoyment from indulging his boyish impulses and having "fun" that comes from games that they enjoy. This is an unrealistic image of a man who never enjoys himself, but he makes a distinction of what games his son should see him play and which games he is still trying to master. Life is a balance and this balance must be effectively mod-eled without glorifying the weakness of the boy as an example of the model of manhood.

"Old school" (and much wiser) parents than too many of us have become took charge of their children's lives and showed them that maturity was authority. Those parents had a time for everything and they didn't let their children stay up all night and do whatever they wanted to do. There was children's space and there was adult space and the two were well defined. Modern parenting has obscured the distinctions in space and time. Many "modern" or "new school" par-ents act as if they are afraid to put their children in the bed or at least, out of adult space after a certain designated time. Men must take the responsibility of parenthood seriously by taking charge of their children decisively. Providing meaningful guidance and leader-ship for the children that you parent is not abusive, it is constructive. Your child may say, "Daddy, I don't like spinach." Tell him to "eat it anyway!" If he has the courage to ask you why, tell him "It's good for you and most importantly, "because I said so!" He may not like it and one day he may choose not to eat it, but as long as he is an inhabit-ant in your house (kingdom), he must do as the king and queen say. When he is no longer in your kingdom, he can go into the desert and find his own kingdom. I'm sure to some "new school" parents this sounds cruel, unusual and impossible! But "old school" fathers built Men and leaders while "new school" fathers build Boys and playmates that too often end up as inmates, remains or cremains.

It was shocking to me in the "old school" days, when I discov-ered that the men and women role models around me from teach-ers to ministers and even family elders engaged in behaviors such as cigarette smoking or consumption of alcohol on even a limited basis. These adult models would rather eat a cigarette than to let one of their students see them smoking. These are not Victorian icons, but they took very seriously the example they had to set for the children. It's easy to condemn historical enemies and oppressors for what they do to distort or destroy our lives and limit our possibilities. The more difficult question is: "What are you doing?" You are the King; you are the Queen for those looking to you for leadership. The best indication that you deserve the right and responsibility for leadership is to exercise leadership over yourself. Nobody should have to stand around and police your behavior. We all know that cigarettes kill us with the certainty of the carelessness of the thoughtless and uncaring cop shooting down black boys in the streets. You know that cigarette smoking will kill you, so you should make every effort to stop smoking them or certainly refuse to serve as an example for the young to start smoking. You know the dangers of uncontrolled use of alcohol, so you should stop drinking it or do it in moderation in environments that will not influence the youth looking to you for leadership. In order to be a Man, a Father, a King in your kingdom, you must take control over yourself. This is the beginning of self-mastery.

In order to establish authority over the appetites in our lives, you must call upon that force of "will power" within our self. That "Will" is the representative of the "Divine Kingship" in our Being (or Kingdom).This ruling force in our minds has been weakened and corrupted by the faulty ideas of being subject to indulging our weaknesses, as we have learned during our captivity in the Western World. This is another flaw of being enslaved in "Egypt" for so many centuries. We must call upon the ancient priests of our Ancestral Kingdoms who still remain buried in the recesses of our being and invite them back to authority over our kingdom as we journey through the desert. Once they regain authority, our bodies become our servants for our higher selves rather than our being enslaved to our flesh. We can do this once we restore our power of self-mastery. When we have reclaimed the power that is naturally ours from rediscovering our real identity as "Men in the image of the Divine," there are unimaginable powers available to us. We were the ones who first came into human mastery and we can do it again, but we must make our exodus through the desert.

Transcending to Universal Consciousness

Finally, the only way that this process can be done is doing one of the things that we came to dislike intensely during our captivity and that is: "doing inner work on ourselves and for ourselves." As enslaved people we learned to despise "work that serviced our masters." We discuss this in considerable detail in another publication, Breaking the Chains of Psychological Slavery. (Akbar,1996). This kind of hard work is necessary for independent businesses. We can't sleep until 10:00 o'clock, leave at 3:00 p.m. and take liberal vacations every three months when you "own the bank." When you realize that the bank succeeds or fails based on your efforts, you must be there before the employees arrive in order to open the door and then spend hours after they have gone to insure that the work has been done. When you own the business, you go home when the work is done. When you run the business, you don't go home until the work is finished. Men and women who own "their business" learn to love each other as man and wife while doing the work and not seeing the work as a competitor for your time and affection. A relationship is work! Sexual indulgence or "the dating game" is easy' it's fun; and it's play. If you don't work on the love relationship, the play isn't fun and games anymore. All things that matter ultimately come down to work! The reason why enslaved people have so many relationship problems and problems of infidelity is because, they don't approach the relationship with the serious commitment of work. They have been intoxicated by the "plantation romantic fairy tales" that makes these relationships always end-up "happily ever after" like a soap opera drama or a music video, rather than the reality of independent commitments and diligent hard work. Relationships like all forms of work require sacrifice by all parties involved. That's what makes them different from "dating games." Each person in the relationship must be committed to doing the work to sustain the "home." You have to clean-up the house when it's dirty, regardless of how "tired you might be." When you're hungry, somebody's got to cook and clean up the kitchen when the meal is over, regardless of how tired you might be. The way to sustain marriages is hard work, sacrifice, self-mastery, patience, belief in who you are and independence as a family. These qualities give you the power to be successful.

You must leave Pharaoh's land and go into the dryness of the desert where there is nothing but sand, bramble bush and briars. There is no water, and nothing to feed life except the source of life (the sun). You must leave the riches of Pharaoh's paved streets, his fountains, his cultivated fields and your economic dependence on him. You must come together with those who made the exodus from Egypt with you and commit to restoring self-knowledge. Everyone who made the exodus has a responsibility in the process. We should not expect the leadership to do all of the work, nor should we think that we only have to passively follow. The call is for all of us to make the exodus: women into womanhood and men into manhood. We must all be initiated into our unique human power—back into our human authority over self. We must survive the challenges of the desert in order to reach the "promised land." The desert is a frightening placing with serpents, snakes, fears of hunger, starvation and even death. In the desert there are agents from pharaoh's kingdom. When you stand up to make the exodus, there is the likelihood of losing your position in pharaoh's kingdom, such as your "job;" loss of pharaoh's favor; there are ghosts in the deserts that make you wonder if you will get tenure or complete your "degree", fear of not getting promoted or hired in pharaoh's corporations. One needs to learn in the desert that: "I can run my own kingdom;" "I can rule my own kingdom." You will have to re-discover that: "I did it first and I can do it again; I taught the rest of humanity how to build and run a kingdom and I can do it now."

The only way this can be done is to come back into the belief in yourself and the Creator who made you who you are. This knowledge gives you the assurance to re-gain authority over yourself and your kingdom. You must overcome the fragmenting influence of egotism and the concept of "I" that was one of the weapons of our captivity. We must restore the ancient conceptual idea of "I am because we are and because we are, therefore I am." Once we come into the awareness of the super "I Am", we have been restored to universal consciousness of the "I Am" who proclaimed Himself on Mount Sinai, "I am that I am." Once that voice reverberates in your mind that you are on "Holy Ground," wherever you are, so take off your shoes right now!

4

Defining Black Manhood

Thinking on the Basis of "Facts"

T he challenges faced by African American Men in this time are some of the most serious challenges that have been faced by African Men since the dawning of civilized life as we know it. Since all evidence suggests that humanity had its origins in Africa, then this represents a rather strong declaration of challenge for African Men. The challenges of prior generations have been ones that were essentially confrontations of physical survival. Even though a manifestation of these contemporary challenges may include physical survival, these are much more subtle because they affect the entirety of our evolved humanity to this point. We certainly don't want to minimize the significance of white-on-black violence or for that matter, black-on-black violence; the most serious threat comes from the destructive and insidious impact of the systemic institutions and principalities of "white supremacy domination" on the planet earth. The system of "white supremacy" is more destructive and specifically directed than simply "racism." Other oppressed people will often generalize from the expressions of "racism" to being religious, ethnic, or even gender discrimination and will equate the systemic process of "white supremacy" to mistreatment of them because of often invisible, behavioral or self-selected categories of human characterization. This system of "white supremacy" is not simply a discrimination against African people because of their physical racial characteristics, but an irrational preoccupation with the insistence of white Caucasian (European) superiority because of their racial/color characteristics. There is both a physical and a metaphysical deeply held conviction that their humanity occupies a higher rank on the scale of human evolution. They assume that both scientifically and theologically that "white" was made to dominate over anything black because of its "natural" superiority and the "natural" inferiority of anything black. African people are a victim of this irrational delusional system of thought. This system of white supremacy actually preceded the brutal atrocities of Euro-American slavery and its aftermath. It was because of this well-entrenched conviction of their God- given superiority that slavery and all of its abominations were inflicted without any sense of moral restraint. If we are aware of these facts, we should never be shocked or amazed at the inhumane treatment that we receive from the hands of people whose fundamental assumption is their natural superiority and less than human inferiority of Black people. We should be appropriately aware and do whatever is necessary to protect ourselves against such inhumane treatment, but there is nothing in the history of our encounter with white supremacy that should make Black people ever assume anything but the worst. Of course, there are deviant anomalies who have historically distinguished themselves from the masses of their cultural belief system. When those deviants have occurred, they have always been firm advocates in helping to protect Black people against the severe abominations of the majority of their people. Whether it was John Brown who gave his life at Harpers Ferry, Virginia trying to free the slaves or more recent instances of white Americans who gave their lives during the Civil Rights struggles, those unusual white deviants have always been firmly convinced that the white supremacy mind set of their people was almost incurable. These white advocates who had grown up within the cultural setting of their own people, were often less convinced of the capacity of that "white mind" to change than were black people who were victims but unaware of how entrenched white supremacy was. Black people are not operating with sound historical facts when they trust that there is a possibility for change in this regard. The Black Men, who operate with facts and in reality and awake from dreams based on hope and forgiveness, would realize that there is no evidence in the history of our contact with white supremacy that it is likely to change. The murders, brutality and deceptions over centuries are evidence of how deeply embedded and destructive is this system of white supremacy. A noble and changed individual is not suggestive of a fundamental alteration of what history has shown to repeatedly return in an ever more vicious and destructive form. This declaration does not require an apology or justification for the genuinely sincere white person who is operating with facts and has a sincere desire to change the circumstances created by white supremacy. It's painful to acknowledge but if we accept the evidence of facts, it seems that white supremacy is the natural orientation of the "racist" predator and his "victimized" prey. This is not accusatory but the only logical conclusion that facts, history and experience can suggest for the long-standing condition of black/white relations. The only logical orientation of black people is to always expect the worst from this white supremacist mind set and to be willing to accept those rare deviations of those whites who salvaged their humanity from the multitudes of those who share their cultural system.

In addition, Black people must acknowledge that they have too frequently internalized the values of "white supremacy" as a self-destructive value system that causes them to devalue themselves and Black Life. The outcome is to condemn and degrade themselves and to attack and distrust the behaviors and the people who have refused to accept this system of white supremacy and its inevitable conclusions of black inferiority. With the internalization of this mind set, Black people often engage in behaviors that serve the purpose of white supremacy by destroying themselves, black men, women, children or families who are struggling to preserve their unique and worthwhile identity as "non-white people." "Self-Improvement" too often means despising ones black or African identity and seeking in whatever way possible to become "white," since this has come to mean "of superior value" and anything that associates you with your natural characteristics: whether it's physical features, 'sane' self-protective behavior or even your distinct concept of moral excellence that has served you well in times of distress. Even the concept of manhood is something that must resemble white conduct or white excellence. These internalized self-destructive values encourage Black African people to destroy themselves, their relationships, and their communities. They look upon Black scholars, artists or any (white supremacist) unauthorized "Black Men" as suspect when they celebrate any quality that would distinguish Black African reality from white people and the glorification of their whiteness. These Black people are viewed with suspicion and considered dangerous if they demonstrate any serious commitment to the affirmation of Black people.

When you combine the outside attacks against Black people coming directly from the overt attacks of white supremacy , with this internalization of white supremacy by large numbers of Black people themselves, it is surprising that there are any Black people still left to restore authentic Black Life. In other words, it's remarkable that there are any remaining examples of Black people left on this planet. The overwhelming numbers destroyed by health/disease problems, unemployment problems, education problems, literal self-murder in suicidal, patricidal behaviors and the mind-altering effect of drug and crime problems are added to these circumstances of self-destruction puts African Black people under siege. The death that comes from poor health/ eating habits, habitual use of destructive drugs (whether legal or illegal) the self-destructive abuse of Black people against themselves represents yet another manifestation of having internalized the "white supremacy" values that help destroy Black life. Black manhood is clearly in danger of becoming obsolete and there are limited prospects for any substantial improvement so long as these conditions persist. The restoration of Black manhood in order to salvage Black life is a necessity or Black African people will become artifacts in European museums. This effort to define Black Manhood represents a critical war to save civilization's oldest example of human life: the African person. This is a "matter of fact" that must guide the vision of those who recognize the reality of this time and the last 400 years of African confrontation with "white supremacy." The above statement is a harsh indictment and the moral fiber of the African spirit trembles at this realization. Of course, the preservers of white supremacy condemn such a statement as "hate-filled" and brutal in its frankness. This must be seen as the conditions under which Black Life has endured for nearly four centuries and it is only with the clear honesty of this context can we begin to effectively evaluate how to change the conditions that confront Black Life. With the clarity of our understanding, there will be a realization of how urgent it is for Black Men to take responsibility for saving what remains of Black Life and fully appreciate the circumstances that we must consider in defining Black Manhood.

Excellence vs. Perfection

It is a romantic dream or a science fiction movie to imagine that the problems faced by Black people are not real. Even with these dangerous prospects and frightening realities, there is a question that must remain uppermost in the minds of those who want to become "Men" and fighters for Black life. That question is: Given all of the odds; given the almost impossible circumstances; given the barriers that would have devastated any other human breed long ago; why are Black African people still here? This question must be confronted and an answer will probably direct us to fulfillment of our Vision For the restoration of Black life. There is nothing wrong with researching and compiling the data and information that point towards Black destruction. In this discussion, we have been actually quite gentle in pointing towards many of these horrific details. The question that confounds all of these horror stories of the last 400 years and continues in the daily news, remains: Why have Black People not been completely destroyed? The "junkies" are not the role models, because they are already destroyed. Those who are warehoused in prisons, without the possibility of parole, for horrendous and murderous crimes against other Black people, are not the models. Those who are the incorrigible perpetrators of black-on-black crime are not the role models. Those who abuse and assault women and children in the black communities can't be the models. Those who disrespect and destroy their own children and leave them to the mercy of chance and circumstance are certainly not the models. But, there are models of excellence that suggest why Black people are still here in spite of all of these atrocities. If we spend all of our time focusing on and studying the deviants, the victims, the abnormal, the devastated, the degraded, we will end up with an image of the destitute, and hopeless Black man. In order to insure the continued survival and restitution of Black life and Black men, then it's important to put our focus on those who did survive and became models of hope and possibilities for others.

This is the rationale for "the definition of the Black Man" that this discussion is concluding with. This definition of Black Manhood will be a collage of unquestionable models of Black Men. These images are not perfect, but they are excellent. They all had their flaws, limitations and not one of them had all of the answers for all of the problems confronting Black Men. I suggest that these are the kind of images that we need to attend to because they all have traits of excellence that will insure Black survival and growth. The rule that should guide our study of these examples of Black Men should be primarily concerned about the excellent aspects, ideas and qualities, worthy of our imitation if we want to become Black Men. We should not waste a lot of time trying to identify their imperfections. We assume that they are not perfect, as no mortal Man of Excellence will be. A serious problem that we too often encounter in our journey to Manhood is to give up the effort when we find the flaws, or some limited form of imperfection. One weakness in our effort to grow as Men is this unnatural dichotomy or separation in our thinking that uses an either/or measure of our models for manhood. In this kind of thinking, either the model is "God-like" (i.e. perfect) or he's disqualified from consideration. This is the easy way out to avoid using the excellent models to identify the excellence in ourselves. It's actually the cowardly "boy's "way out of the growth process into manhood. When we look at our models of manhood with a moral magnifying glass, we will always find some imperfection. Once we discover that our "model" drank too much on some occasion or engaged in "boyish" conduct in his journey to manhood, we are ready to disqualify all of the Manly achievements that he brings to teach us because he is a male, boy, who is evolving to Manhood. We have a much distorted notion of what it means to be a human being. Many Christians would not accept the human side of "Jesus the Christ" if he had not been presented as born of a Virgin. They have this distorted notion that he could only be a perfect man because he was born in absolute "purity," and this qualified him to be the good man that he became. It also lets them escape their responsibility to be good as men because they were not born of a Virgin. This leaves them completely free to give up their responsibility of cultivating their full human development of seeking the excellence that all men have.

So the rule of this study is not to look for a perfect model born of a virgin. Whether it is the five men that will be discussed in these examples that I have chosen in this discussion of "defining manhood," or models that you select in your journey towards manhood, we must focus on the excellence that they demonstrate and discard the remainder. These five examples of models of Black manhood are not the only Men who could qualify for this discussion. They are five men who have impacted my growth and the growth of thousands of other "boys" seeking their manhood. There is recognition that each of these Men, who I find to be models of excellence in one or more aspects, also has flaws that I try to share to the extent that my vision permits me to see. Certainly, there are limitations of where the flaws actually outweigh the "excellence." As developing Men, we must decide where that balance is, and as we grow in our Vision, we may find that the excellence is contaminated by the flaws, but we want to study to see if the excellence can provide guidance to our search for the excellence in our Manhood.

The Courage of Martin Luther King, Jr.

The basic battle strategy of "non-violent resistance" that was selected by Dr. Martin Luther King, Jr. for confronting "white supremacy" is a strategy that I personally disagree with. I respect his philosophy and rationale for selecting this strategy. The presumption of a developed and functioning conscience on the part of one's enemy would appear to be a major premise for this strategy to work. As we've discussed in earlier parts of this book, the historical record does not seem to support the presence of such a conscience in those who victimized Black people with such brutal and inhuman abuse. My sense of self-preservation would oppose letting such brutal people attack me and those I loved until their apparently flawed "kill-switch" of conscience was activated. There are settings where ones enemies or captors do have a conscience that would activate in the core of their humanity at a reasonably early point to intervene in their brutal treatment. Even when they recognized that they were armed with superior weapons, their conscience would activate with a sense of guilt and they could not brutalize the weaker enemy or captive in such an inhuman way. They could not bomb children in the act of worship or perform acts of violent torture against the elderly and the infirmed simply because they had superior strength to demonstrate. Non-violence as a strategy might work to deter the attacks of a humane enemy who had the capacity to see your shared humanity. For an example, the strategy of non-violence would be an excellent approach to resolve disagreements between factions of African people. The assumption of a mutual respect for the humanity of the factions and the act of forgiveness could quiet hostilities between people who both had a sense of moral conscience. This was not the case of the "white supremacist" enemy who did not see a common humanity that they shared with African Black people. I don't believe this strategy worked in changing the social order for Dr. King, but it was attributed with greater effectiveness when in fact, the rise of those who believed in "Black Power" and were willing to die in their self-defense became increasingly vocal. Recent revivals (during the first quarter of the 21st century) of publically espoused bigotry and actions of a conservative judicial system confirm that the racist zenophobic hatred that confronted Dr. King has simply been dormant during the illusion of progress in racist attitudes and policies. The fear of well-deserved retaliation forced the "white supremacist" to attribute superior power to the non-violent strategy because of fear of retaliation from the alternative.

A fact that cannot be denied and stands out in the conviction of Dr. King's implementation of his strategy was his outstanding courage. Dr. King exemplified among modern African Men, the most remarkable capacity for such courage. The kind of courage that he showed is the kind of courage that enables a man to stand firmly as a Man on the basis of faith in his beliefs, whatever they happen to be. One cannot be a Man without Courage. It isn't simply the bravery that permitted him to confront the cruel and atrocious cops and their vicious dogs of Birmingham beating down unarmed women and children. It was the courage that gave him the daily power to confront the possibility of death at the hands of those who had no respect for his life or the lives of Black people. "Courage" was the character trait that fueled such bravery. His belief in his mission and the power of his conviction is the courage that makes a man of unquestionable excellence.

The power of Dr. King's courage permitted him to confront even those who were his colleagues and peers who had so internalized the same devaluation of Black life that he had to resist their desire to step down and let the enemy win. The middle class educated Blacks who had gained so much by internalizing white supremacy that they could not find the courage to stand by the conviction of their cry for freedom. One of the most revealing writings by Dr. King was his "Letter from a Birmingham Jail" when he confronted his middle class cowardly colleagues, preachers, teachers, fraternities, lodges and so-called educated 'negroes' who were willing to let him suffer in jail in support of the "white supremacist" enemies. Everyone claims him as their hero once he received the Nobel Peace Prize and was legitimized by "good white folks" and then martyred, but it was the courage that fueled his ability to even confront his own people is the remarkable trait. When he took the protest to begin to confront the injustice of the Viet Nam War, even his Black bourgeois companions begged him to keep it quiet and not make the "higher white powers" angry. Dr. King never had a successful civil rights campaign in his hometown, alma mater and the current location of his martyred monument in Atlanta, because there were too many comfortable 'negroes' who did not have the courage of conviction that he had. He found a more loyal following who responded to his courage in the back woods of Alabama, Mississippi and rural Georgia who had nothing to lose by confronting the white supremacist system with his challenges to oppression. He couldn't get the semi comfortable, status quo, educated "Negroes" (with a capital 'N') living and working in the "post-slavery" version of the plantation house, to get into the streets and challenge the system. He had to get the people who didn't have any stake in the economy or the system to walk in the streets and to challenge "white supremacy." Since he was a product of this group in so many ways, it took real courage to challenge them to stand up for change. Once he received acceptance by the power holders who dreaded the consequence of the rising tide of "Black

Power" and chose Dr. King's non-violent challenge instead, then the other "house negroes" began to join ranks with him. After the "white stamp" of approval was given and the most serious dangers had past, then came the negroes: teachers, doctors, preachers, lawyers and all of the others joining arms and singing "We Shall Overcome". They jumped in the front of the line and tried to take over the movement. Before this approval from the owners of the house had legitimized King, these same Negroes identified Dr. King as a troublemaker and a "rabble rouser". They were disturbed about him going around the country "stirring up trouble" when they thought they had things relatively good. Because of Dr. King's courage and persistent conviction, the movement grew, gained strength and transcended the realistic fears of retaliation from the "white supremacy system."

Dr. King, then, presents us a graphic example of a man of courage and the power that courage has to transform a social movement. He confronted his people's historical enemies of slave masters and white supremacists and then confronted the weak and passive fear that had been internalized by his peers and colleagues. It took courage to confront the enemy within and the enemy without and this is an example why this quality is such an important one in defining manhood. Men stand up with the courage of their conviction to fight the enemies of himself and his people. Courage means that you are willing to be different and ask hard questions and confront vicious enemies. Courage gives you the power to be extraordinary rather than ordinary and to leave the boys doing boyish things when you take on the challenges of manly building. Courage equips a man to be unusual, exceptional and to stand up when everyone else is sitting quietly down. It took courage for Dr. King to take his Boston Theological Education out of the classroom and into the streets. His training had prepared him to conduct the business of church and theology in a building, but courage propelled him to take the church into the streets to confront the enemies of his people. Courage empowered him to imitate the image of Jesus by confronting injustice in this world at that time. The eloquent stories of Jesus never depicted him as having a palatial, place of comfort to meditate on high ideals. Just like Jesus, Dr. King walked in the streets, along the seashore, in the fields of Mississippi, Alabama and rural Georgia; he was a courageous "trouble maker" confronting the pious 'holier than thou" religious and political leadership. Yes, he had the educational and social credentials that would have let him comfortably sit inside and avoid confrontations, but Dr. King had the courage of a man who had the conviction of the courageous man, described as Jesus.

On some level Dr. King understood that a man had the responsibility to use the power of his convictions to transform this world and not wait for the metaphysical and mysterious "rapture" to magically bring about human and social transformation.

Within the context of this discussion, perhaps this "New Vision of Manhood" may be going far beyond the scope of this book, but I will borrow some of Dr. King's "courage" and reach beyond anyway. I believe that religion is not intended as a passport with a first class ticket to heaven, but as a guide to help Man transform earth into a more heavenly place. This is what I think we saw in King's conviction, determination and persistence by taking the church into the street. We lose the inspiration of his example when we begin to deify him as something more than a man. There are some people who have speculated that Dr. King had a "Messianic" mission with a special calling from the Divine that gave him his particular power of leadership and courage. There is much greater value to his legacy if we think of him as simply a man who fulfilled his development and his potential that all men have to some degree. He was a fully developed Man in the sense of his evolution and he used his particular gifts as Imhotep used his gifts of full development and designed the earliest step Pyramid in Kemet (or Egypt). He was the kind of man of gifted musicians like John Coltrane or Charlie Parker who found music beyond the ordinary. He was the kind of humble man of George Washington Carver, humble and submissive and found secrets of plant growth by simply walking through the fields of Tuskegee, Alabama and reading the plan of creation. King was the kind of man who had the courage to let his conviction take him to a new level of human possibility. He was compelled by the same force that pushed the vanguard of human evolution at the base of Mount Kilimanjaro to declare that he wanted to be more than just an animal, but a Man and he stood up and saw what other animal life had never seen before. It's that same spirit that is in every Man who develops a vision and it manifested in Martin Luther King, Jr. to move beyond being a "boy" and lying down as a defeated male. Perhaps with uncertainty of where he was going, he stood up and became what he was born to become. It took courage to confront the fears of restraint and convention and took the church into the street and transformed freedom from a concept to a movement. In doing so, his life became a lesson of one of the qualities of becoming an African Man and that lesson was the power of Courage.

The Defiance of the Honorable Elijah Muhammad

Another remarkable man that I would suggest we should study to emulate if we want to become real African Men is "The Honorable Elijah Muhammad." His example, instruction and direction made some of the most outstanding men of modern time, such as: Malcolm X, Muhammad Ali and Louis Farrakhan. From all accounts, up until the day that he died, Malcolm X (Al Hajj Malik Shabazz) always gave credit to this Man for making him the Man he became. Anyone who has studied contemporary development of Black political Power over the last century has had to pay tribute to the influence of Malcolm X (who was literally named by his Teacher and Mentor, The Honorable Elijah Muhammad.) There are few who can question that the gold standard of Black Manhood of the 20th Century was Malcolm X. Since I certainly agree with this designation of Malcolm X, the reader might wonder why he is not identified specifically as one of the examples in this definition of Black Manhood. It's a part of the effort to confuse the thinking of our growth that popular history, media and mythology would seek to obscure the source of such excellence and instead elevate the product or student. What's even worse is the tendency to negate the influence of Elijah Muhammad in building men by giving greater credit to his student than to the teacher, even when the student himself was loyal and consistent in attributing his transformation to Elijah Muhammad. Stories of the vilification and angry separation of the student from his beloved and highly respected teacher was done almost deliberately to obscure the significance of Elijah Muhammad in building men. The same is true for the elevation of Cassius Clay above the person who literally named and generated the mind of the man, Muhammad Ali. Only Louis Farrakhan has remained adamant about the source of his manhood and directed the generation of his fame to its rightful origin, The Honorable Elijah Muhammad. Our understanding of truth and fact requires us to be as accurate as we can to restore this correct definition of manhood. This is not intended to minimize the specific talents and genius of these three examples of Elijah Muhammad's most highly esteemed students.

It was the mind of manhood of Elijah Muhammad that transformed the "boy" called "Detroit Red" from the cocoon of prison and the streets of his potential destruction that would have prevented him from ever emerging as the Iconic butterfly, Malcolm X. Even though, Al Hajj Malik Shabazz continued to grow as a Man once he was transformed, he never departed too far from the MESSAGE TO THE BLACK MAN (Muhammad, 1965) that came from his spiritual father and teacher, The Honorable Elijah Muhammad. Actually, my initial exposure to Elijah Muhammad and what he represented as a man came from the highly articulate words and penetrating communication of Malcolm X (Malcolm X &Haley, 1964). But as I studied the life, words and works of Malcolm X, I was directed to the source that had made Malcolm X, the impressive man that he had become. There was no other organization, leader, university, church, mosque or temple that was taking boys who were nobodies and making them into men who were somebody. He did not come with the skills of ordinary theological seminaries, social and behavioral science or educational skills but he did more than the best of those institutions in the transformation of thousands of Black Men. Elijah Muhammad touched the lives of the social rejects—chronic alcoholics, junkies, prostitutes, recidivist criminals and social outcasts who the best of the best had pronounced as hopelessly lost and successfully transformed them as examples of the highest form of "Manhood." He built an economic empire that the best schools of business and economics could not produce with these human "castaways" as his team. He had an international education system, a weekly national newspaper paper before USA Today ever came into existence. His organization owned factories, clothing stores, a bank, and farms and was importing food from around the world before the sustainability movement was even conceived. His followers were "eating to live" before anyone was talking seriously about the relationship of health to the food that people ate, particularly within the confines of the Black American community. Activities that have become commonplace in nearly all health conscious environments of all races and religions since the beginning of the 21st Century was already commonplace as a part of the life style of Elijah Muhammad's organization in the middle of the 20th century. Elijah Muhammad must be seriously considered as a remarkable man and an unquestionable example of what Black manhood has to mean. Without any consideration of analyzing or proselytizing into his religious theology, wise people have to honestly study and consider what kind of man was so capable in building Black Men?

This characteristic of defiance captures a limited but crucial aspect of what I believe is essential in understanding the example that Elijah Muhammad brings to the definition of manhood. Mr. Muhammad firmly believed in a man's right to define himself. Addressing the Black people's need to reclaim their manhood, he declared that, "it is better to be called 'X' rather than carry the name of Williams, Smith or any other name given to Black people during their enslavement." He said that it is better to be an unknown (X) than to choose to carry the slave master's name. He firmly believed that the first step towards authentic liberation was to rid oneself of the plantation name that was given to Black people. He suggested that eventually "you'll discover who you are and take on some name that came from your own Land, but in the meantime just be 'X'. Many of the people who adopted his teachings were in communities where there were people with multiple given names such as John, Malcolm or William. Even though these names were not original African names, he permitted people to keep them as names selected by their families for them, while discarding the family name that identified you as the property of someone else. As a result, depending upon the time of your arrival into the community where you studied under his direction, you might be John X , John 2X, or John 12X . . . . etc., in order to distinguish you from the earlier John's who were a part of that community. (As further indication of the lifelong commitment of Malcolm X to the teachings of Elijah Muhammad, he adopted the original name, "Shabazz", even after the alleged alienation between the student and his teacher that was not an Arabic name but one taken from the metaphysical teachings of Mr. Muhammad.) It's interesting to note that even though Elijah Muhammad, adopted the family name of Muhammad for himself, the Arab captivity of Africans did not escape him, so he maintained his family "given name" of Elijah throughout his life as he distinguished himself from -the apparent contradictions of shifting from one captor that was Christian with an Islamic religious group associated with Arab captors. This issue of the Arab and Christian captivity of Africans was often used to undermine the logic of Elijah Muhammad's teachings. There were many subtleties such as his name that indicated a much greater depth to his understanding than many people gave him credit for. However, this is not the subject matter of this discussion but the issue of defining oneself was a very important aspect of the restoration of a people's manhood and there was no single African language and ethnicity that would restore the Black man to his original identity.

Elijah Muhammad defiantly went ahead to redefine everything about himself and his students. He introduced a unique admixture of dietary laws that were partially Old Testament Hebrew Kosher Laws, Islamic (Halal) Laws, Hindu Vegetarianism and an array of restrictions that were intended to counteract the influence of 400 years of poor dietary habits from captivity and poverty in rural Southern

American culture. He even anticipated restrictions in the Western diet that it's taken nearly 50 years for European American nutritionists to identify. He redefined Black history and began to advocate that the Black Man of African was the "original man" before paleontologists, geneticists and anthropologists began to confirm this from the fossil records and their genetic research. This redefinition of history completely altered how Black people saw themselves as actually the parents of the human family. This idea and conception of our origins on the planet completely redefined the Black relationship to human civilization. Despite the attacks of European historians when he began to introduce this idea to his followers and the submissive disbelief of those enslaved African people who had been educated by whites, Elijah Muhammad was defiant in his version of the human story and determined to demonstrate the significance of people defining themselves despite the oppositional arguments. In his defiance he demonstrated that if you are going to be a Man, you must be willing to name yourself, define your place in human history, advocate for your definition of reality and accept nobody else's definition unless it is compatibly consistent with yours.

According to Elijah Muhammad, Men stand up and defiantly declare: "This is my reality!" Knowledgeable Black people become very upset when they read European history books, see movies or television programs where white men, for an example, declare Greece as the originators of civilization. This is the reality that white men declare for themselves because that's what Men do. White men in these instances, wrote the book, made the movie and required that other people accept it because Men define reality consistent with their own needs. You should certainly seek to tell the truth but men have a right to do research, select the information that is relevant to their empowerment and place themselves in the center of their reality. Such defiant determination to define himself and put the Black man back in the center of what was relevant for them was typical of the process of self-definition and self-determination of Elijah Muhammad. He firmly believed that in order to empower yourself , you must know yourself. "Knowledge of self," he said "is the key to power." Here was a Black man, speaking and teaching to Black men, women and children who had been systematically robbed of their power to define through enslavement and to claim the knowledge of who they were. I don't know if he knew the hidden message written over the portals of the Ancient African Universities at Karnak in Ancient Egypt over 5,000 years ago that instructed the entering students, that the code to learning and human power was and remains:

"MAN KNOW THY SELF." The same key was adopted by the Greek invaders several centuries later when they entered Africa and were amazed by the advanced culture that they could not have imagined before seeing Ancient Egypt (Kemet).

Mr. Muhammad succeeded in modernizing this Ancient African directive for building Men and was able to motivate ex-convicts, life-time criminals, non-readers and self destructive social misfits to be motivated to read, build and explore for self-definition. His students developed self-respect and re-discovered the full human capacity of respecting others. He taught them the same sense of defiance that was demonstrated by Malcolm X , Muhammad Ali and hundreds of others that "this is a Man talking; you respect me and the woman with me and I will respect you." He taught his students that people could not disrespect him and the woman with him and expect his respect. Just as he taught the man to respect himself, he also taught the woman to respect herself in order for her to demand respect. The basic principle that he insisted upon was: "You must respect yourself if you want to be able to demand respect." He dressed up his followers in the most dignified and modest dress regardless of their circumstances; he cleaned up their habits of self-demeaning and self-destructive conduct, whether it was smoking or drinking in public or engaged in loud, boisterous and profane talk. The formula worked. Men or women could walk in the most unclean environments dressed in their excessively dignified dress and demeanor and even junkies on the streets or homeless alcoholics would step aside and attempt to brush themselves off as if someone of royalty was passing by. People would see the Sisters of the Nation of Islam coming by and would quiet their public profanity and behave like gentlemen by opening doors and trying to improve their appearance if only for a fleeting moment. The obvious radiance of self-respect of the men and women that had been transformed by Elijah Muhammad had a positive influence on the self-respect of the people they encountered. They recognized something was different about Mr. Muhammad's transformed people. Even though many African Americans were frightened of the defiant confidence of these people, they respected them and recognized that these were people who knew who they were and admired their dignity.

People were very curious about Elijah Muhammad's students. They wanted to know where did they get that "defiant" self-confidence that gave them the audacity to go everywhere on street corners and door-to-door with those Muhammad Speaks newspapers published under the guidance of Elijah Muhammad with weekly features of his sermons of "Message to the Black Man. What made Elijah Muhammad bold enough to say and do whatever he wanted to say and was capable of instilling that defiance into Malcolm X, Muhammad Ali, Minister Louis Farrakhan and so many of his students? How could he stand up and boldly call the "white man" the "Devil" in the 20th Century in America and not suffer any direct consequences? Of course he was despised and defiled by white men and their passively socialized enslaved trained students trapped in "boyhood." But, it was the power of self-knowledge, self-respect and the defiance to define oneself and ones reality. Once you have those ingredients of human power, you can do what you want to do—that's a Man! Elijah Muhammad turned his people away from "white dependence" and into "Black independence." He demanded moral excellence and self-discipline. He was firm in his idea that you cannot change the world if you don't begin by changing and controlling yourself. If you are dependent on alcohol, tobacco and illegal drugs then you are subject to the legal and personal consequences of giving them control over your life. Despite the accusations against him for having multiple wives, there was considerable evidence that he followed African cultural practices and the cultural and religious laws well-defined in the Jewish and Christian laws that authorized providing for and supporting as many wives as you could provide for and treat fairly. He understood the requirements of manhood and maturity that led him to restrict such worldwide polygamous practices among the formerly enslaved Black people in America who had been so alienated from their own culture and civilization for so many centuries. Rather than the serial polygamy and infidelity that is so characteristic in Western culture, he enforced a level of restraint that would be consistent with the image of moral excellence that he was trying to instill in his followers.

Mr. Muhammad was defiant in his determination that Black people had as much right as any other people to define themselves for themselves. It didn't matter how bizarre the story might appear to other people, he assumed the right and authority to present it as "Black Truth." It was nobody's business if he decided to present a story of "ships" from outer space that were there in service to the Black Man then that was his business. He had as much right to formulate his own mythology as any other people had a right to create a mythology that exalted who they were. No one argued with the right of white people to describe UFO's seen by some of their reputable scientists as within their right to speculate about the unknown.

So his claim that there were "Mother ships" from outer space that some Black scientists were aware of but most people and no white people had ever seen, then that was within his right of self-definition. If there were widely accepted white scientists who argued then (and even now!) that there are certain invisible genes operating in the human brain that makes white people intellectually superior to people of other colors, then he was within his rights to present a story suggesting that a scientist named Yacub, (not found in white history books) engaged in scientific experiments to develop a race of white mutants so incredibly barbaric in their inhumane treatment of other people on the planet that they were outside the realm of normal human variation. There certainly was considerable evidence of white behavior that invited some type of explanation. Mr. Muhammad was defiant in his right to define the reality as experienced by Black people for themselves, rather than accept the perpetrators' speculative stories about the justification for their barbaric and inhuman treatment of people of color and even of each other.

The Jewish religion is a voluminous narrative of their suffering at the hands of oppressors (gentiles) since the earliest days of Hebrew recorded time. That is absolutely their right as Men to define the reality of their historical journey over time. In fact those who deny the Truth of their suffering and reality of their most recent holocaust are considered to be "holocaust deniers" and co-participants with the most vicious violators of their humanity or even contemporary participants in their holocaust experience. They have a variety of "holocaust" museums in several American cities that insure that the story of their suffering should never be forgotten. This is the right and responsibility of men to protect the narrative of their story. Elijah Muhammad strongly emphasized the repeated and consistent recitation of the suffering of Black people so that the story of the African holocaust or "maafa" (Ani, M., 1994) would never be forgotten. Black people are told that they should "get over the atrocities of slavery and its aftermath" since it happened "so long ago". No one would dare tell the Jewish people they should "get over their suffering" when the former occurred on American shores and the latter events took place in Europe. People respect Jewish Manhood and their right to tell their story but do not have the same respect for African Men to tell their story. Minister Farrakhan, Malcolm X and so many others who simply wanted the African story told from the Black perspective have been condemned as "militants, racists and demonic trouble-makers."

We should have absolute respect for the Manhood of Jewish people to define and defend their story. An indication that African people have not had their manhood fully restored is the failure to tell the story of Black suffering from the Black perspective. The fact that Black people accept the dismissal of scholars and teachers who defiantly persist in telling the story of Black suffering as "militants" who should be ignored is indicative that that our Manhood is not intact. Africans are not men, because Men make sure that horrors from the past do not repeat themselves or they are willing to die trying to insure that such atrocious behavior will never occur to their people again. The Jews are absolutely correct when they declare "Never again!" This is a declaration of Manhood regardless who is disturbed by the declaration. Every generation of Black youth should not have to relive the oppression, injustice and atrocities of previous generations, if Men are being developed. This is why Elijah Muhammad's defiance is a model for manhood because it defies the atrocities of the past, creates images in the present and protects the unborn from any similar pain occurring in the future.

The Commitment to Knowledge and Expanding Vision of W.E.B. DuBois

Dr.W.E.B.DuBois was probably the most outstanding and productive scholar of the last century, who devoted nearly his entire life to the issue of self-definition of Black people. He was undoubtedly one of the best examples of the significance of knowledge as a characteristic of Manhood. The courage of Dr. King, the defiance of Elijah Muhammad, the pursuit of knowledge by Dr. DuBois are outstanding examples of the best of what it takes to be a Black Man. As we have discussed earlier in this chapter, these men are not being presented as examples of "human perfection" but each demonstrated "excellence" in the qualities that we are highlighting. From his earliest education to his death at 95 years old, he was constantly seeking answers to understand and resolve the issues confronting Black people in the world. His writings, his research, his teaching and his scholarship were unrelenting in his effort to resolve the difficulties and restore to the highest level of human excellence for his beloved African people. He was devoted to expanding the "self-knowledge" of Black people as the instrument for resolving the centuries of oppression and captivity they had suffered. From the rural southern United States as a student and teacher at Fisk University and later as a Professor at Atlanta University to the lofty centers of European education such as Harvard University, The University of Berlin or the

University of Pennsylvania, his mission was consistent and that was to seek the knowledge that would bring freedom to Black people. In the course of his 90+ years, he went through a variety of organizational, social and political efforts to eliminate or radically change the course of African captivity and oppression.

His earliest days were devoted to the process of trying to eliminate racial segregation as the most visible example of persisting oppression. This led to his participation in the organizational efforts of the "Niagara Movement" that created the NAACP. Even his efforts there were focused on developing "The Crisis Magazine" which was a tool that was geared primarily towards cultivating self-knowledge rather than racial mixing, that soon became the primary focus of some of his fellow founders. Interestingly enough, he devoted his efforts in other arenas when knowledge was no longer the primary objective for the "Advancement of Colored People". As we trace the journey of his life, we find that knowledge remained his essential mandate for transformation right up until his final assignment by Kwame Nkrumah, first president of the newly independent Nation of Ghana, to spearhead the editing of an Encyclopedia Africana that he was working on at the time of his death and repatriation to Ghana, West Africa. This ultimate move back to the continent of Africa where he died and is buried today is another indication that he was guided by the light of knowledge and neither ideology nor passion, which had alienated him from The Honorable Marcus Garvey who advocated a "back to Africa movement" that Dr. DuBois had firmly opposed earlier in his life. His transformation as a man was always guided by knowledge as the ultimate determinant for action. The significance of knowledge as the quality of excellence that Dr. DuBois demonstrated is probably captured in this brief quote by him in his "Address to the Country" in 1906 in Harper's Ferry, West Virginia where he proclaimed: "We will not be satisfied to take one jot or title less than our full manhood rights." This is consistent with our reason for identifying Dr. W.E.B. DuBois as one of the best illustrations for excellence in this "vision" for the full attainment of Manhood by Black People.

Dr. DuBois' dedication to the establishment of Pan Africanism with his numerous efforts to organize African people all over the world towards the common objective of restoring "Black Life" is another concept that his scholarship (knowledge) led him to reach. His knowledge expanded his vision and he saw the problem of Black People to be more than a regional problem but a problem that was of global proportions. He was convinced that the problems of Black People would have to bring together the entire African world in a full commitment to resolving those problems. As we have observed above, he began by trying to address the race problem on a local level with his early efforts to organize the NAACP, but this vision expanded to see the race problem as being one that could not be solved by a "civil rights campaign" in North America as was the initial objective of this well-intended early venture. The impact of slavery in the Americas had its continental parallel with colonialism in Africa. There are many critics who argued that Dr. DuBois was in disagreement with the "back to Africa movement" of the Honorable Marcus Garvey and they in fact had considerable disagreement with the implementation of Garvey's UNIA strategy. Dr. DuBois' commitment to Pan Africanism and his ultimate repatriation to the African continent demonstrate that his connection to the significance of Africa in the Liberation of Black people to be an essential part of his "Vision." As observed above, Garvey was driven by the "passion" of returning to Africa and DuBois was guided by study and organization to address this ultimate objective as his own life demonstrated. There is considerable evidence that the effort to bring together the African world in a common intellectual and organizational thrust to resolve the problems of Black people would appropriately identify Dr. DuBois as one of the "Fathers of Pan Africanism," and an ally with the essential principle of Marcus Garvey.

Dr. DuBois' commitment to effective leadership guided by knowledge was the source of another of his controversial concepts: "The Talented Tenth" and the organizing of the Boule' or Sigma Pi Phi fraternity. This concept was thoroughly consistent with his considerable reverence for knowledge as the guiding light of human excellence. He meant by this phrase: "leadership of the Negro race in America by a trained few," was not an elitist denigration of those who were not academically "trained." The criticism of "Dr. DuBois as an elitist, was based on the distorted implementation of his idea by those who thought that he "had in mind the building of an aristocracy with neglect of the masses." This couldn't have been further from the truth as he firmly admonished those who had misapplied his call for the "intelligent leadership who would need a thorough understanding of the mass of Negroes and their problems for which he emphasized scientific study." As he stated in his memorial address criticizing the distortion of his concept: "Willingness to work and make personal sacrifice for solving these problems was of course, the first prerequisite" of this leadership group. In this same address, he further declares (consistent with this writer's argument for excellence): "We cannot have perfection. We have few saints. But we must have honest men or we die. We must have unselfish, far-seeing leadership or we fail." (Quoted in Lewis, 1995, pp. 349-350.) He was very critical of those college-trained self-appointed aristocrats who were more committed to personal gain and reputation than to the collective struggle and guidance of those with lesser skills. He attempted to clarify his regard for knowledge as the criteria for excellence and leadership of this "Talented Tenth" in the same address where he states: "In a day when culture is comparatively static, a man once grounded in the fundamentals of knowledge, received through current education, can depend on the more or less routine absorption of knowledge for keeping up with the world."

He saw the knowledge that he called for in this "Talented Tenth" and in himself as a dynamic process subject to change and readjustment with the discovery of new information. This is the kind of Knowledge that we call for by choosing Dr. DuBois as an example of this characteristic of excellence that builds true manhood. The knowledge that he exemplified wasn't a static earned degree in a frame on a wall among a Man's mementos or the early pages of his resume' but a tool that was constantly being modified from the mastery of fundamental skills of literacy until in his case, he was laid to rest some eight decades later in a mausoleum in the coastal city of Accra in Ghana, West Africa. Ones legacy should be guidance for those to follow to use the path of knowledge that you have found to continue the journey that you have inherited.

The Self-Sufficient Economics of Booker T. Washington

There is definitely a great deal in Booker T. Washington's overall philosophy of his concept of Black Manhood that I strongly disagree with. As we look for these qualities of "excellence," it's important to keep in mind our introduction to this section that emphasized the significance of "Excellence" and not to be distracted by a search for "Perfection" as we look at these models for the development of Black Men. Mr. Washington's vision for economic development represented one of the best examples and most successful that Black People have had. His strategy was more successful in transforming rural Black life than any single strategy since the captivity of Africans in America. This strategy moved the former Black captives from the economic dependency that two centuries of enslavement had produced towards a degree of independence that still has not been fully duplicated in actual practice. It began to move Black people from a "share-cropping" system of economics that depended upon the former captors towards a level of self-sufficient control of their own material environments that has still not been fully realized in over a century since. Booker T. Washington believed in institution-building as foundation for economic self-sufficiency. This example of his strategy does not debate the benefits of a socialist as opposed to a capitalist system. It simply addresses how to succeed in a capitalist system without being subjected to the servitude of the successful capitalist. In order to build institutions that you control, one must have access to capital. The development and construction of schools to teach the youth how to become men requires capital. The production of food, health care and manufacturing requires capital. Transportation requires capital; money requires capital and in a capitalist system, even life itself requires capital. In order to construct and organize an economic system that replaces capitalism requires capital. Even though Dr. DuBois' knowledge and that of many others envisioned an alternative system, they remained dependent on the resources of capital to do their research and to travel the world and see alternative systems at work. Booker T. Washington was very clear that you had to have resources that you controlled in order to establish independent institutions. This argument does not dismiss the abuses and misuses of capital and the problems of (so-called) "capitalism," it only identifies the realities of being in a system that requires capital to do almost anything, successfully in it. With this understanding, Mr. Washington organized a central organization of Black Business Men, which was called the National Business League. For many years, this was the central organization for the Wealth of Black Americans. Their primary objective was not political but to quietly bring together a network of Black wealth to serve as the major funding source for independent Black institutions. There was a diversity of political opinions and philosophies, but under the guidance of Booker T. Washington, they came together as a central unit of wealth for Black development. Unfortunately, they didn't have the collective wisdom and vision of DuBois' "Talented Tenth" but they were organized around their capacity to generate wealth and serve as a foundation for Black capital development. This type of independent organization was an example of Washington's economic strategy that would serve Black people well in this millennium, if it was successfully duplicated with the insights of Mr. Muhammad, Dr. DuBois and even the courage of Dr. King. Wealth with a collective vision of developing economic independence cancels out the negative qualities of greed and selfishness that often accompanies capitalist systems.

Another impressive aspect of his strategy was his concept of self-sufficiency in Institution building. Tuskegee Institute which he founded and served as its president for many of its formative years was a model of this self-sufficient institution building. Every brick for every building, every board for every building came from the land that surrounded the school and was built with the skills of the students who attended the school. The food was grown in the gardens of the Tuskegee grounds, and the milk came from the cows in the Tuskegee dairy. The student uniforms were made in the tailor shops and the laundry was done in the campus laundry. This aspect of Institution building and self sufficiency was very consistent with the "defiant philosophy" of Elijah Muhammad who insisted that the path to manhood was that the "Black man must do something for himself." Booker T. Washington and Mr. Muhammad, probably could not have agreed on too much else, but they firmly believed that you cannot wait or expect for those who were your former captors to insure that you had the basic necessities for life. This doesn't eliminate the moral responsibility of those who took life from you to assist you to regain your livelihood. It is inconsistent with the actual reality of the Black experience of having been made a captive to assume that their captors might engage in morally responsible conduct. This doesn't suggest that every man should "pull himself up by his own bootstraps" as many contemporary political conservatives would argue, while being in denial of the reason "why you don't have any boots to pull yourself up with." They want to blindly deny that slavery and oppression took away your boots and your straps for self-sufficiency. Certainly Mr. Muhammad's "defiance" never permitted him to forget this but he had no expectation that this moral act of repair would ever be forthcoming from the former "slave masters" and continuous oppressors. From all indications, Mr. Washington chose to deny the reason for Black economic deprivation and blamed Black deprivation on personal deficiency in the motivation and education of the Black man. So even though he arrived at the same conclusion of the importance of self-sufficiency as did Mr. Muhammad, they differed on the explanation for how the Black man got in that condition.

This deviation between Mr. Muhammad and Mr. Washington about the origin of the Black man's condition probably resulted in the strong disagreement of Dr. DuBois and Mr. Washington about the solution for vocational education for self-sufficiency. Dr. DuBois argued that "the object of education was not to make men carpenters but to make carpenters men" (S.DuBois, 1978). Men were thinkers, leaders ("The Talented Tenth") and this was the path to human freedom. Black people did not need an education that only prepared them to do what slavery and captivity had perfected in them and that was to engage in vocational skills, but the proper use of those skills and the recognition of the source and the reason for the deficiency was the objective of education. Unfortunately, there was no reason for serious disagreement because both Mr. Washington's self-sufficiency and Dr. DuBois' call for enlightened and committed leadership were not at all in contradiction. We can only speculate but there is reason to believe that the marriage of the two ideas found expression in the formulation of Pan Africanism which was a strong component of Dr. DuBois' alliance with President Kwame Nkrumah and the establishment of the independent government of Ghana under his leadership.

Self-sufficiency was an important principle from the model offered by Booker T. Washington. This ability for people to provide the basic necessities of life for themselves should be an essential aspect of Manhood. It doesn't require a "separatist" notion of going off and living away from other people, but it does require the kind of autonomy that doesn't leave you to depend on other people to provide food, shelter, clothing, healthcare and the basic requirements for human survival. This kind of autonomy provides people with a sense of self-respect in the human community. The captivity of Black people has not been in such ancient times that they should forget the cost of such total dependency. Even more recently, there are those living in these times who recall how Black Professors, Doctors, Lawyers and successful businessmen were not able to use their financial resources to find lodging, adequate transportation, healthcare and even food because of well-established ("Jim Crow") laws that prohibited them from going into those "For White Only" establishments. They would often have to travel many miles and endure insults from those with fewer financial resources to locate a place to eat, sleep or obtain transportation where "Coloreds were allowed." Even in this time that has been called by some: "A Post Racial Society" (with Black participation in white political systems), have too quickly forgotten that at the end of the Civil War during the period called Reconstruction, Black people had more political power and presence than is present in Post Millennial America. There were Congressmen, Legislators, governors, and political figures in greater numbers than is even present in this time (the early years of the 21st century). Even with a Black President in the White House in the 21st Century, we have seen a level of disrespect for Black life and achievement, not even shown to a homeless man who was a part of the self-sufficient white captors. Without self-sufficiency, in less than ten years after the troops were removed out of the Southern United States to enforce Reconstruction, the level of Black political presence in the Congress, the Courts and State Governments was reduced to such a level that it took nearly a hundred years to gain even limited Black presence to be restored. Without the legitimate transformation that comes with the establishment of authentic Manhood, of which self-sufficiency is a part, the clock could be turned back, yet again in this 21st Century.

There is meaningful instruction in the lives of the Jewish people. They maintain an emphatic motto of: "Never Again!" Their experiences of not taking participation without self-sufficiency for granted taught them a painful lesson that Black people should learn from. They understand that as long as there is one anti-Semitic person on the planet there is always the possibility of another Adolph Hitler and another Holocaust. They are adamant when they even suspect that someone might be advocating anti-Semitic thoughts. A good example is their vehement opposition to Minister Louis Farrakhan, who made reference to "unrighteous people who claimed to be Jews, Christians or Muslims." The passing mention of any Jews in any negative context made them claim that the Minister was the incarnation of the modern "Hitler/Devil". Minister Farrakhan's objective was to awaken Black people to the importance of knowing that there can be dangerous people masquerading in any religious costume, but all that some of his critics heard was the negative reference to the word "Jewish" and he became the world's worst anti-Semitic person of the century. It's possible that my reference to this incident and the mention of the Jewish people in connection with Minister Farrakhan could get me identified as an anti-Semite, when I am celebrating the Jewish people as an example of vigilant people who understand the importance of realizing how easy it is to be taken from privilege to oppression when you have not fully developed your critical vision. The argument being made is that being self-sufficient in providing for yourself, defining yourself and identifying your enemies is an admirable quality that is well-demonstrated by the Jewish people. Black people should define who is racist and anti-Black and they should not ask permission for this right.

It is certainly admirable for well evolved human beings to choose a moral "high ground" and achieve the capacity to forgive ones captors for their oppression. From my perspective, it compromises the lessons that must be taught to future generations when forgiveness gets elevated to actual celebration of one's oppressors. The Late Governor George Wallace became a shining example of resisting the humane treatment of Black people during the Civil Rights Struggle in the 1960's. In fact, his devaluation of Black Americans and opposition to humane treatment and respect for Black Life became the cornerstone in his campaign when he ran for President of the United States. Some years later when the world around him had changed, he changed and expressed regret for his conduct. This transition resulted in Tuskegee Institute (as it was called at the time) an iconic symbol of Black education in Alabama awarded him an Honorary Doctorate degree. It's very difficult for me to imagine a Jewish University in America or in Europe awarding an "apologetic and reformed Nazi" whose conduct condoned the death of Jewish people an Honorary Degree or any other form of celebratory tribute. Even though acceptance of the flaws in human conduct and their capacity to change and apologize is a noble act of moral transcendence, there is an implicit distortion of the historic record for those who will come behind and lose the transformative power of memory that sustains the vow and commitment to "Never Again." To forgive your enemies is noble, but to celebrate them is self-destructive and disrespectful to the lives that they destroyed. (But this discussion is a digression and it evolved while reflecting on the admirable "excellence" of Booker T. Washington, who as I have repeatedly reminded the reader, like all of the men in this section, was not perfect and that does not discredit the qualities of excellence that are present in all evolved Men.)

The Uncompromising Integrity of Paul Robeson

Paul Robeson (S. Robeson, 1981) is the last example of Black Excellence that should definitely stand as a prime example for the many Black Men of outstanding artistic talent and achievement in multiple disciplines, whose athletic achievements or fame for entertainment sometimes blinds them to their authentic Manhood. To be recognized by ones enemies and ones people as exceptionally talented and who is able to achieve outstanding success in the use of one's intellectual, artistic, athletic or whatever exceptional talents they may have is a real challenge to achieving this "New Vision of Manhood." Paul Robeson's significance is that he achieved fame in not just one field of outstanding accomplishment but in multiple fields. He was a star collegiate athlete that in this time could have surpassed many Heisman Trophy winners, Gold Medalist in the Olympics and other platforms of fame that have even become more visible with the enhanced media exposure and exaltation in this period of the early 21st Century. He refused to let himself be limited as just a "brute gladiator" for the entertainment of his audience though he excelled on the football fields, and the basketball courts. He put aside his athletic achievement and made it secondary to his academic achievement and left undergraduate school to reach comparable heights in Law School. He subsequently excelled as an actor and then created a new bar of excellence with his vocal music talents. He was as philosophically sound as he was musically talented. He was creative, profound and humble. With all of that achievement in one human package, he refused to be defined or have his people devalued by the desire of some people who wanted to isolate him as an exception of excellence in these fields. He was approached and made outstanding offers to play the role of a demeaned former slave, but he refused to compromise his excellence in exchange for solitary rewards. Hollywood and Stage Directors offered him outstanding personal rewards if he would agree to play roles that showed Black people in demeaned and devalued roles. He was told that he shouldn't be dignified on the stage or screen but instead that he should mumble his words like a semi-retarded field hand. His producers tried to get him to be inarticulate and play the role of servants and clowns and they would reward him with great personal wealth and esteem. Mr. Robeson said, "I will not do it". They said to him, "Then you won't act." He said, "Well, so be it, I will not act then." They retaliated by doing all that they could do to limit his exposure as the man of distinction and talent that he was. They wanted him to show his talents only where and how they wanted them displayed but he insisted that he was a free man who should be able to go wherever on this earth that he wanted to go. They said, "We will take your Passport, limit your exposure and make you a prisoner in the country of your birth." He said, "All right, I still will not stop thinking what I think and I will stand for what I believe and I will not participate in the devaluation of my people, no matter what you do." Even with his mobility restricted, he refused to limit his mentality as a Man. He was determined to be true to the gifts that he had been given and was uncompromising in his integrity.

Wouldn't it be great if we had more Men of talent and genius like Paul Robeson, who refused to compromise their integrity for fleeting financial rewards and recognition by their former enslavers? Suppose we could get all of the "Star Athletes" to think like Paul Robeson: to refuse to kick, run, pass, shoot or hit another ball; to refuse to play another sports game until there were investors, managers and agents in comparable proportions to their numbers as players in their sport? Suppose that there were athletes who so valued Black Institutions that they would not play another game for the NFL, NBA or even Collegiate sports until there was a guaranteed proportion of the profits earned committed to the endowments of Black Colleges and scholarships for deserving Black Students in every profession where Black people were under-represented? Suppose that they would refuse to play another game until funds were set-up to finance the research to determine the health, wealth and social disparities of Black Americans and the communities that they came from? Suppose they would refuse to play for any university that did not have a serious and equally uncompromising staffed Institute to study African culture and insure the dissemination of that information? Suppose all the actors, entertainers, rappers, comedians, dancers and vocalists would demand that some of the studio profits be channeled to improving the lives of the people in the communities who looked like them? When they achieved platinum sales, Emmys and Oscars, they would not speak another line or sing another song or dance another dance until the dying communities that gave birth to them were as famous for producing future generations of talent like theirs rather than obscene commercial wealth, drug abuse and decadent fashions. Suppose they had so internalized the image of Manhood exemplified by Paul Robeson, they would refuse to take a movie or television role that did not reflect positively and constructively on the lives of Africa and African people. Suppose that they had the "uncompromising integrity" that they refused to be role models that devalued Black Life by playing roles that advanced ugly or derogatory images of African people? Suppose they were more concerned about the impact of their role on young Black viewers than they were about personal fame or wealth? Suppose that these image-makers vowed, as did Paul Robeson, that they would be dignified in their portrayal of Black life or they would be invisible as image makers, despite their talents and personal material sacrifice? Suppose they were determined to do what was best for the masses of their people, regardless of their personal loss for taking such a stand of integrity and dignity?

Again, no one is without blemish or imperfections, but they could follow the suggestion of Malcolm X who said, "They don't have to hang their dirty laundry on the line outside for all to see." If Black Men have problems, we can find ways to "clean our laundry at home." We don't have to post our madness on social media for the world to comment on and let "garbage collectors" make millions of dollars distributing our dirty laundry. If we have disagreements (as all men do) let us disagree behind closed doors and not on the evening news for public consumption. Our problems with each other are our problems and Men must take responsibility to recognize those problems, and work to correct them without jeopardizing the integrity of the entire community. This is how Men who understand the difference between the illusion of perfection and human excellence address the flaws in their humanity. The energy behind this capacity is the uncompromising integrity of Paul Robeson who saw himself as an agent for the excellence in Black Manhood and for his people. Every talent, and skill that Men have is a gift for their people and they must struggle to use it for the collective good and for the yet unborn who will look to them as models of Manhood. Personal greed and egotism must not compromise the integrity of your Manhood, no matter how talented or gifted you may be.

Paul Robeson was a man of multiple talents and unquestioned genius who was uncompromising in the use of those talents as a positive expression for the uplift and improvement of African people throughout the world. His integrity in this regard was non-negotiable. Even though he was almost unable to make a living for himself and his family at periods in his life because of his firm positions on how his talents should be used he would not portray Black people in demeaning ways. He turned down many acting roles and performance opportunities and because of his political commitment to transforming the social order for the benefit of African people, he suffered tremendous retaliation from oppressors, who wanted him to renounce his ideals. In spite of this he was still able to delight the world with his irrepressible gifts and talents. He might have been able to reach much greater heights in the entertainment world if he had been willing to compromise his integrity. He stood by his values and made the sacrifice of personal wealth and fame. His legacy is not only the mark of his angelic talents, but his example to Black Men of the importance of sacrifice. It doesn't matter what you might profit from a certain situation, a Man must ask what will this require of me in terms of principles? Men must be willing to answer the question of: "What will this require of me in terms of values?" What will be sacrificed if I act in contradiction to my highest values?" "What price will it cost my children and my people if I am unfaithful to my

Truth?" "Are you willing to make that sacrifice for your Truth? Paul Robeson was because of this quality of Excellence he possessed as an African Man.

The "Chosen" People

Every people's "Cultural Story" is part historical fact, part traditional narrative and part myth. Each cultural story is a metaphor for human development in its entirety. That means that every people (Chinese, Japanese, Ashanti, Russians, Arabs, Yoruba, Greeks, Bantu, Zulu, and Hebrews) all have an allegory or a narrative about the human, spiritual, physical and psychological development of the human family. For many people in the Western World, the Hebrews or Jewish People have presented their Cultural Story as the story of human development for all people at all times and at all places. The struggles and the evolution of human development that is described in the Torah or Old Testament of the Bible are presented as the total picture of all humanity. In fact, this is only their "Cultural Story" which reflects their record of their development as they have described it. They have had a very powerful impact on many different people (particularly in the Western World) and have used their historical allegory or metaphor as the universal picture through which many cultures have come to view their development. There are undoubtedly universal elements in their "Cultural Story" that are true for all of humanity. In their story they speak of periods of their defeats, victories and oppression in captivity using either Babylon or Egypt as the setting for their "story." They have described Babylon or non Jewish people (called Gentiles) as a culture of oppressors and enemy forces to their development, who imposed their cultural story and divinities on them. In other places of the Jewish Cultural Story, they say they were "captives in a strange land for over four hundred years" and they were forced to do slave labor and suffered great hardships of building someone else's civilization. This sounds like the same story that happened to captives from Africa in America. Probably both stories have historical accuracies as well as myths and both people have a right to tell their "Cultural Story." Perhaps this is why when the African Ancestors heard the story of Babylon captivity and Egyptian Slavery; they were able to identify with the story as their own. When Africans were freed from captivity and they heard the story of Babylon, they could tell their story of slave ships that took them from their homeland to Virginia, Alabama and Mississippi. When the former Jewish captives speak of mean evil kings called Pharaoh, Africans could speak of mean Governors like

Ross Barnett of Mississippi and George Wallace of Alabama. When they tell about the Pharaoh who refused to let their people go from captivity, Black people should tell about Robert E. Lee and other Confederate Generals who fought to the death to keep their people in captivity and Heads of States who resisted permitting them their human freedoms and live as free human beings. The "African Cultural Story" is as valid for Africans in America as was the Jewish Cultural Story in the land called Egypt.

When you invoke and tell your "Cultural Story," you declare your earned place in the human family and can show your development, your challenges, your strength and resilience. You can reassure the developing youth of your strength and refine the "New Vision of your Manhood" that the path of excellence always wins. No matter what opposition you may encounter, sooner or later, Truth, Righteousness, moved among the people and began to stir in the consciousness to bring into fruition a "Joshua" who will down the walls of Jericho or a Nat Turner or Frederick Douglas to break the chains of bondage. It's important for men to know that unjust bondage does not last and the forces of Truth begin to move in the consciousness of the collective mind of the people and the appropriate force to remove captivity is eventually born. The struggling, striving, persistent mind of the captives seeking a solution for their problem create one who may be raised in the house of Pharaoh who will restore them to their "Promised Land" of human prosperity and dignity. The one who takes the form of Moses in one "Cultural Story" leads the people to freedom. This archetype of Moses occurs in all People's Cultural Story because what makes you the Chosen People is that you "choose" God's Way. It's not a special brand that makes you the "chosen ones," it's the active process of being the right "choosing people". When you choose Truth, you become "Chosen". Once you are "Chosen" you become propelled to your own freedom, liberation and exodus.

A New Life Will Come Forth from the Womb of Darkness

Once a Man begins to choose the Truth of his own reality and begins to build from the bricks of his own "Excellence," as DuBois did; as Robeson did, as Elijah Muhammad did (and his students: Malcolm X, Louis Farrakhan and so many others did); as King did and as even Booker T. Washington did, you are emerging into the full growth of the butterfly and the freedom that this brings. What qualities did all of these African Men have in common and shared with fully evolved Men of every culture? First of all, they demanded respect for the Women of their people. They all had a fundamental concern about the importance of building families to insure the continuity of their Communities. They understood the significance of working together and the value of Unity. Of course, each man was different, and there was certain to be disagreement, but they shared a commitment to their People. They all understood that freedom does not come as an achievement by yourself. They all struggled in the "desert" during the exodus to freedom. They shared a commitment to the children coming behind them, not just their children but the children of their People. This wove together the fabric of family in the highest sense of the word. They understood that all the Women were the Mothers and all the Men were Fathers and the children belonged to them all. This generated the sense of excellence that we have described for each of them.

Secondly, they all had faith in God or some Higher Power that transcended their mortal and temporary work in this plane. Their concept of a Higher Power was of a transcendent reality that was so much larger than the limited names and characterizations that their mortal experiences had permitted them to glimpse. Even though only some of these Men devoted considerable time trying to identify characteristics of this "Deity that rules the Universe, set it spinning through space, maintains and sustains it on firm principles of Truth and self-sufficiency; that brings life out of death and transforms what appears to be death into a higher form of life." They respected the common language of Nature and Time and Timelessness. Even though these Men were identified with distinctly different religious or secular belief systems, they had a fundamental faith in the transformative power of a Higher Reality. The same belief in a Superior Being to transform reality was shared as much by Elijah Muhammad who called himself a Muslim as by Dr. King who called himself a Christian. When you deal with the essence of the commitment of these Men, you begin to understand that the arguments about denominations or ideologies were irrelevant and they were all committed to the freedom of the humanity of their People. Only the most superficial of boyish disagreements were about what name to call the Superior Power. You may call Him (or Her) by any name that is meaningful to you. If you don't know what "Allah" means, don't use it; if the name "Jehovah" doesn't mean anything to you, then don't use it; the same is true for Yahweh, Ja or even "God," (if your perception is of a mirror image of that word is "dog". If your studies have given you access to the name "Obatala" as that power is called in Yoruba or "Nyame" by the Ashanti of Ghana or "Amen-Ra" in Ancient Egypt (Kemet), "Ausir"(Osiris) or "Auset"(Isis), use that name to address that force that awakens your connection with that Higher Power that is the Master of Transformation and guidance for Manhood. The important idea that we need to grasp is that in order to be Men in the order of these Men who provided leadership to Freedom is that we must be respectful of certain Universal Principles of Truth, which all of these Men held to.

A third quality that all of these examples of Black Manhood had in common was a recognition and respect for the power and importance of Moral Values. They understood and believed in fundamental principles of Morality: "To want for their Brothers what they wanted for themselves;" "To do unto others what they would want others to do unto them." Again, none of them was perfect in His conduct, but they all believed in Moral Excellence as an objective. Each one had his own fallibilities, but they were still "Excellent Men" doing the best they could with their human imperfect forms. Even though they may have come short of achieving the standard that they believed in, they stood for, represented and did their best to live up to principles of Moral Excellence. Flaws exist in all of us, but we must be accepting of the efforts in ourselves and other men to achieve this standard of Moral Excellence. If any of us was perfect, there would be no growth because we would already be the Divine Higher Being, but none of us is perfect so we all must strive to become something better and this guides our growth and transformation. Each of these Men in his separate form of excellence understood that the Freedom and continued growth of African people is fueled by a belief in principles of moral excellence. When we speak of Moral Excellence, we don't mean a long list of disciplines that must be followed or some type of "holy purity" that only a human that had not grown from an animal could live up. The moral excellence that suggests that these Men strived for is the respect for the highest of human values as we mentioned above: "To strive to treat other humans as you would want to be treated." Nearly every religious system that I have encountered has a value that is very similar to this Moral Ideal that is called in Christianity: "The Golden Rule." In fact, one does not have to embrace a religious system because it is found among all civilized humans in all parts of the earth. It seems that this principle of being considerate of others is what separates Men from Beasts. It's not surprising that these African Men of Excellence would be guided by this level of Morality.

The fourth thing these Men of Excellence shared was the significance of history and the commonality of all African people (called Pan Africanism by most)as the context for their strategies. They understood to a lesser or greater extent, but at some level that the African experience must be understood in an historical context. They all had a fundamental understanding that there was a connection between Egypt, Johannesburg, Harlem and Montgomery. They had an appreciation for the connections formed by history between Ethiopia, Cincinnati and Kingston. They had a feeling for the interconnection between Mali, Songhai, Timbuktu, and San Francisco, Chicago, Dallas and Milwaukee. They understood that there were fundamental similarities between the struggles in South Africa, South America and South Miami. Perhaps they didn't share the geographical and political analysis of DuBois (with the companionship of Robeson) as he formulated the call for Pan Africanism; Dr. King was clear about the threads that ran between apartheid in South Africa, and the struggles for freedom in Selma and Birmingham. Elijah Muhammad chose a banner head logo for his newspaper with the Black man reaching from Africa over the Atlantic to lock hands of Unity with the Black man in North America. All of these men in, various ways, understood the connection of African people all over the planet and their work was directed towards building that unity. Even Tuskegee University that was built by its founder, Booker T. Washington, (with its confused analysis in awarding an Honorary Degree to George Wallace, that was discussed earlier) has historically had more African students among its student body than many of the other more politically more progressive historical Black Colleges and Universities. (Of course, the first Independent African Presidents of Nigeria (Azikwe) and Ghana (Nkrumah) were graduates of Lincoln University in Pennsylvania, which is another example of the significant relationship between Africa and the historical Black colleges in North America should be noted as indicative of the long-standing relationship between Africans in America and Africans on the Continent.) But, within the context of these Men of Excellence, it's particularly noteworthy that despite the relatively more conservative political philosophy of Booker T. Washington, he recognized the significance of Nigerian and Liberian students as a part of the International network of African people. This is simply another illustration that even when this idea was not an explicit part of their work, they all had in common the recognition that African people must be united with African people wherever they are. There was a clear perception that the oppression of African people was a worldwide problem that needed to be addressed regardless of different specializations of

Excellence in the "New Vision for Black Men". This suggests that a part of the consciousness of being a Black Man is to be fully aware of the relationship of African people, historically, economically and politically.

Finally, all of these Men of Excellence valued Black Life. They did not apologize for being Black. They did not buy into those who accused them of "reverse racism" because of the love they had for their people. They believed in the human being, they believed in human power, dignity and freedom, but they believed in the humanity of their people first and foremost. There is nothing wrong with loving and valuing oneself and being committed to insure that your people are free from oppression. Real Men believe in themselves because that is what propels them to do for themselves rather than depend on someone else's hand-outs. Concern for others and the totality of the human family is appropriate after you have sustained and done for yourself. Once you have established and assured your freedom and power as a human being, then you are adequately equipped to help other people attain their rights as human beings. This is the way that fully developed and evolved Men think.

So how do we use these examples of manhood and recognize adequately developed Men? The process of becoming Men requires that we try to find the "Excellence" in ourselves and to model ourselves after these examples of "Real Black Men." We must seek out the many examples of similarly outstanding models of True Manhood. We must study the lives of Men of Excellence, such as these and celebrate them in our environments with pictures and examples of their achievements. We should have pictures on our walls of Paul Robeson, Elijah Muhammad, W.E.B. DuBois and willingly share their stories with anyone who inquires as to why we display their pictures. Popular entertainers, sports figures and media heroes shouldn't be celebrated simply for their superficial talents and popularity, but for the depths of the Manhood that they represented. There are many others like these men who we have noted in this discussion, such as The Honorable Marcus Garvey, Muhammad Ali, Malcolm X, Nelson Mandela and so many others. They should share wall space with Mary McCleod Bethune, Sojourner Truth, Harriette Tubman, Madame C.J. Walker, Ida B. Wells and the kind of True Black Women who represented the same values in Womanhood that paralleled these values of Black Manhood. It's important to structure our environments in such a way that we are constantly reminded of the best we can be, not just in fashionable physical appearance, but in the essence of what truly makes us the People that we should want to be. Once you identify these images of Excellence, you will say without thinking: "I want to have the intellectual brilliance of a Dr. DuBois who never lost the focus of seeking to find a way to use his intellect to uplift his people. I may not have the natural talents of a Paul Robeson or the natural intelligence of a DuBois, or a James Baldwin but I want to find my "Excellent" talents and use them for something more than personal fame and fortune. Your evolution into Manhood will drive you to become as much like the models you admire as you possibly can. You will want your legacy to be one that states that you gave your life for African people just as these models believed and sacrificed for us. This doesn't mean that you long for death, even though you don't mind sacrificing your life to achieve the greatness you were born for. The mind of the True Man should be one that is driven to live for his people and to realize that he has immortality in their elevation. He realizes that he must emulate, he must identify with the best and he must educate. This is the fulfillment of the evolved "butterfly" that emerges from the cocoon as a soaring expression of beauty, brilliance and power. Every time we get an opportunity and can get the attention of an audience, the True Man should be teaching what he has learned. These Men have a responsibility to let all who they encounter know that civilized life began in Africa. Let them know the Legacy of Ancient Egypt and the Nile Valley Civilization. Let those who don't know become acquainted with the greatness of Songhai, Timbuktu. Let them not mistake the origins of the world's introduction to the concept of a Higher Spiritual Being (God) was established by African Men who found their origin and shared it with the world. Out of respect for those Ancestors who brought us into life, we must let those who do not know that the cycles of life and the passages of being, the foundation of numerology that gave birth to Mathematics and the qualitative and quantitative connection of the symbolism of numbers came from the teachings of African students of Nature and Life. There is no arrogance in celebrating our astute African ancestors who sat at the feet of the Created World (such as the Dogon people) and saw the arrangements of stars that contemporary generations are only now beginning to appreciate and explore. These African Ancestors were the Wise Men who saw stars in the Eastern Sky and predicted reality that it has taken centuries to confirm. These were patient Wise Men who sat and studied the stars and read the timeless and universal messages written on the tapestry of the sky. They understood the cosmos by carefully observing the microcosm and understood the spheres and cycles of time. They looked at the caterpillar, saw the cocoon, marveled at the butterfly and read the universal formula of transformation of human consciousness.

After we emulate (identify), and educate we must celebrate African Men of Excellence. We should not have just one holiday a year for one Man, instead we should make everyday a holiday for African Men of Excellence. These daily celebrations should not be parades, marches or a day off from work but they should be celebrated by displaying their pictures, reading from their writings, listening to their words and should decorate our environments to celebrate their greatness. Just as other people display their Men of Excellence on their money, in their places of respect and learning, African People should know them as a part of their daily lives, so that the "Boys" will know who they should seek to emulate. We should sing the songs of Dr.King's greatness and memorize the powerful words of Elijah, Malcolm, Ali and Garvey. We should debate the ideas and programs of Booker T., DuBois and remind every generation of the sacrifices of Robeson and the values that he stood for. Forget about Santa Claus and the Easter Bunny and instead create images to seal in the memory of those who brought freedom to African minds and restored African humanity. This power to emulate, educate and celebrate African Men of Excellence and to internalize their best characteristics will transform Black Males into Black Boys and Black Boys into outstanding Black Men. Once African Men know what Manhood is, then they can once again begin to be "husbands" to African Women, fathers to African Children and dependable leaders for African People. When African Manhood is restored, there will be a New Life produced out of the womb of darkness where it was whirled around for a numerical time of "9" and the "9" was transformed into "1" and the "1" emerged (head first) into a world with waiting hands of knowledge (10), lighted by reason to synthesize the New Vision of "3" formed of physical, mental and spiritual cosmic substance. This New Life will take the world again to universal plateaus of understanding, learning and being that will transform all of reality. As Men of Africa, did it before, they will do it again!

Selected Bibliography

Akbar, N. (1995). *Natural Psychology and Human Transformation.* Tallahassee, FL: Mind Productions and Associates.

Akbar, N. (1996). *Breaking the Chains of Psychological Slavery.* Tallahassee, FL: Mind Productions and Associates.

Akbar, N. (1998). *Know Thy Self.* Tallahassee, FL: Mind Productions and Associates.

Alexander, M. (2010). *The New Jim Crow: Mass Incarceration in the Age of Colorblindness.* New York: The New Press.

Ani, M. (1994). *Yurugu: An African-Centered Critique of European Cultural Thought and Behavior.* Trenton, NJ: African World Press.

ben-Jochanon, Y. (1970). *African Origins of the Major Western Religions.* New York: Alkebu-Lan Books.

Blyden, E. (1887,1992). *Christianity, Islam and the African Race.* San Francisco: First African Arabian Press.

Diop, C.A. (1974). *The African Origins of Civilization.* New York: Lawrence Hill & Co.

Diop, C.A. (1991). *Civilization or Barbarism: An Authentic Anthropology.* New York: Lawrence Hill & Co.

Du Bois, S. G. (1978). *DuBois: A Pictorial Biography.* Chicago: Johnson Publishing Co.

Du Bois, W.E.B. (1961). *Souls of Black Folk.* New York: Dodd, Mead & Co.

Jacque-Garvey, A. (1986). *Philosophy and Opinions of Marcus Garvey.* San Francisco: Julian Richardson, Associates.

Griaule, M. & G. Dieterlen (1986). *The Pale Fox.* Chino, AZ: Continuum Foundation.
Haley, A. & Malcolm X (1964). *The Autobiography of Malcolm X. New* York: Grove Press, Inc.

Hurry, J.B. (1978). *Imhotep: The Egyptian God of Medicine.* Chicago: Ares Publishers, Inc.

James, G.G.M. ((1954). *Stolen Legacy.* San Francisco: Julian Richardson Assoc.

Karenga, M. (1993). *Introduction to Black Studies (2nd ed.)* .Los Angeles, CA: The University of Sankore Press.

King, M.L. (1963). *"Letter From a Birmingham Jail."* Birmingham, AL: Southern Christian Leadership Conference.

King, R. (1990). *African Origin of Biological Psychiatry.* Germantown, Tenn.: Seymour –Smith, Inc.

Lewis, D.L. (Ed.) (1995). *W.E.B. DuBois/A Reader (1sted).* New York: Henry Holt and Company, LLC.

Muhammad, E. (1965). *Message to the Black Man in America.* Chicago: Muhammad Mosque of Islam, No.2.

Nobles, W.W. (1980). *African Psychology: Toward its Reclamation, Reascension and Revitalization.* Oakland, CA : Black Family Institute.

Lane-Poole, S. (1886). *The Moors in Spain.* New York: G.P.R. Putnam and Sons.

Robeson, S. (1981). *The Whole World in His Hands.* Secaucus, NJ: Citadel Press.

Toure', A.S. (1975). *The African Intelligentsia in Timbuctu.* New Orleans, LA: Edwards Printing Press.

Van Sertima, I. (1976). *They Came Before Columbus.* New York: Random House.

Van Sertima, I. (Ed.) (1986). *Great African Thinkers (vol.I): Chekh Anta Diop.* New Brunswick, NJ: Transaction Books.

Woodson, C.G. (1933,1990). *The Miseducation of the Negro.* Trenton, NJ: Africa World Press, Inc.

Woodward, C.V. (1974). *The Strange Career of Jim Crow.* New York: Oxford University Press.

Wright, B. (1986). *"The Psychopathic Racial Personality".* Chicago: Third World Press